love yc **12**

THE STORY OF
POP MUSIC

POP HISTORIES

MATT ANNISS

W
FRANKLIN WATTS
LONDON•SYDNEY

First published in 2013 by Franklin Watts

Franklin Watts
338 Euston Road
London NW1 3BH

Franklin Watts Australia
Level 17/207 Kent Street, Sydney NSW 2000

Produced by Arcturus Publishing Limited,
26/27 Bickels Yard, 151–153 Bermondsey Street, London SE1 3HA

Text: Matt Anniss
Editors: Joe Harris and Rachel Blount
Design: Paul Myerscough and Keith Williams

Picture credits:
Corbis: Bettmann 10t, Earl & Nazima Kowall 17t, Ross Marino/Sygma 19b, Robert Matheu/Retna Ltd. 9t, Michael Ochs Archives 12, Denis O'Regan 21; Dreamstime: Kristina Afanasyeva 28, Imagecollect 18; Getty Images: CBS Photo Archive 6r, Hulton Archive 13b; Library of Congress: William P. Gottlieb Collection 5b; Shutterstock: Christian Bertrand 31, S Bukley 5t, 13t, DFree 25t, 26l, Dotshock 4, Helga Esteb 24, 26r, Featureflash 1, 20b, 23b, 25b, 29l, Jaguar PS 19t, Patricia Marks 11t, Music4mix 22, Joe Seer 23t, 27, 29r; Wikia.com: ReapTheChaos 8; Wikipedia: Archivey 16, Beaucoupkevin 17b, CBS Television 6l, 15b, Colgems Records 9b, Angela George 11b, Goaliej54 20t, Roland Godefroy 7, Jimieye 17c, Heinrich Klaffs 14, Robert L. Knudsen 15t.
Cover images: Amazon: top centre right; Corbis: MAXPPP/PATRICK CLEMENTE main; Shutterstock: Efecreata Photography top far left, Featureflash top centre left, Debby Wong top left; Wikipedia: CBS Television top far right, Colgems Records top right.

A CIP catalogue record for this book is available from the British Library.

Dewey Decimal Classification Number: 781.6'4

ISBN 978 1 4451 1867 3

Printed in China

Franklin Watts is a division of Hachette Children's Books, an Hachette UK company.
www.hachette.co.uk

SL002671EN

Supplier 03, Date 0513, Print Run 2378

CONTENTS

THE PRE-HISTORY OF POP

The story of pop music is the history of the changes in attitudes and technology that defined the twentieth century. It touches on other forms of entertainment, fashion and fads. More than anything, it is the story of music that people love.

Music hall

Up until the early part of the twentieth century, the only way to enjoy music was to listen to it being played live. The most popular style of entertainment at the time was 'music hall'. Music hall concerts mixed performances of popular songs with jokes.

TIN PAN ALLEY

The popularity of music hall created a demand for new songs that could be performed by the scene's top singers. Because of this, a thriving song-writing industry developed. In America, it was based around a street in New York nicknamed 'Tin Pan Alley'.

Recorded music

In the early part of the twentieth century, two inventions began to change the nature of the popular music scene. The first was the gramophone, a machine that allowed people to listen to music recorded to pressed plastic discs, known as records, in their own home. The second was the radio.

THE GRAMOPHONE, WHICH HELPED POPULARISE RECORDED MUSIC IN THE EARLY PART OF THE TWENTIETH CENTURY, WAS THE FORERUNNER OF THE RECORD 'DECKS' USED BY CLUB DJs.

Radio stars

Until cheaper record players became available in the 1950s, radio was the most popular way of listening to music. Top singers from the music hall scene could become big stars if they featured on the radio. Being on the radio helped to sell concert tickets.

THE FIRST POP STAR

Radio helped make Frank Sinatra the world's first pop star. During the 1940s, Sinatra's records sold in huge numbers. He was a larger-than-life character with a distinctive singing style. He was so popular that he soon started appearing in films.

Groundbreaking star

Sinatra was hugely popular with teenagers, who had previously shown little interest in music. It was a groundbreaking change. In years to come, teenagers would become the driving force behind pop music.

SINGER FRANK SINATRA WAS ONE OF POP MUSIC'S FIRST GLOBAL STARS, AND WENT ON TO STAR IN A NUMBER OF SUCCESSFUL FILMS.

ROCK AROUND THE CLOCK

Frank Sinatra may have been the world's first pop star, but pop music as we know it began in the 1950s. It was British journalists who first began using the term to describe the decade's most popular form of music, rock and roll.

Rockin' revolution

Rock and roll was different to other forms of popular music that had come before. It was loud, energetic, dancefloor-friendly and was based on black American music styles such as rhythm and blues and jazz. In the mid 1950s, it emerged from America and took the world by storm.

At the movies

It wasn't a particular song or singer that popularised rock and roll. Instead, it was through the films *Blackboard Jungle* (1955) and *Rock Around the Clock* (1956) that most teenagers discovered rock and roll.

RICKY NELSON STARRED IN HIS FIRST FILM AGED SEVEN, BEFORE GOING ON TO MAKE HIS NAME AS A CLEAN-CUT, ALL-AMERICAN ROCK AND ROLL SINGER.

FOLLOWING THE SUCCESS OF HIS FIRST SINGLE, *THAT'S ALRIGHT MAMA* IN 1954, ELVIS PRESLEY QUICKLY BECAME KNOWN AS 'THE KING OF ROCK AND ROLL'.

Sales boom

Rock and roll was the first style of popular music to increase the sales of both record players and the records themselves. Teenagers wanted to be able to listen to their favourite rock and roll songs at home. Record shops began to spring up all over America.

Singles life

In the past, records had been expensive and didn't sound very good. Thanks to the recent invention of the 7-inch single – a cheap record featuring one song per side of the disc – rock and roll records could be made, sold and bought cheaply. Sales of records skyrocketed.

POP CHARTS

During the 1950s and early 1960s, the music industry grew faster than at any stage before or since. To keep track of record sales, pop charts were set up. Like they do today, the pop charts listed the top-selling singles.

First pop hit

America's first number one was *Poor Little Fool* by Ricky Nelson. It topped the Billboard Hot 100, in August 1958. Since then, over 1,000 different songs have topped the American pop charts.

PLAYLIST
1950s POP MUSIC

Bill Haley & the Comets – *Rock Around the Clock* (1955)

Elvis Presley – *All Shook Up* (1957)

Ricky Nelson – *Poor Little Fool* (1958)

Chuck Berry – *Johnny B. Goode* (1958)

Johnny Horton – *The Battle of New Orleans* (1959)

THANKS TO CATCHY SONGS LIKE *JOHNNY B. GOODE*, CHUCK BERRY BECAME ONE OF THE FIRST BLACK AMERICAN ROCK AND ROLL STARS.

ON THE BOX

The popularity of music with teenagers during the early years of pop made TV producers sit up and take notice. TV was still in its early years, but gaining in popularity. Soon, TV would play a huge role in creating pop stars.

Good for everyone

In the 1950s, TV producers were looking for ways to attract more viewers to their shows. Booking pop acts made sense, as it guaranteed that teenagers would tune in. It was good also for the pop acts, as millions of potential record buyers would hear their songs.

VARIETY SHOWS

To start with, pop acts began appearing on popular variety shows, which mixed singing and dancing with comedy and impressions. It wasn't long, though, before TV networks began to set up their own dedicated music shows aimed at teenagers.

The forerunner of MTV

Fronted by a former radio DJ called Dick Clark, *American Bandstand* was the world's first dedicated pop music TV show. It first aired on ABC in 1957 and featured teenagers dancing to pop records and performances from leading singers.

Top of the Pops

The success of *American Bandstand* inspired a British version, called *Top of the Pops*. Both shows played a key role in promoting pop music to TV viewers over the next 40 years.

Star makers

Appearing on TV shows had the potential to turn pop acts into huge stars, particularly in America. The Beatles become stars in America almost overnight following their appearance on *The Ed Sullivan Show* in 1964.

Monkee magic

The runaway success of pop group the Beatles inspired a 1960s American TV comedy about a band, called *The Monkees*. The four members of the band were actors, rather than musicians, but the songs they recorded for the show went on to be huge pop hits.

PRESENTER DICK CLARK, SHOWN HERE WITH BAND THE GO-GO'S, BECAME ONE OF THE MOST FAMOUS FACES IN AMERICA THANKS TO HOSTING THE POP MUSIC TV SHOW *AMERICAN BANDSTAND*.

LIVING LEGENDS

THE MONKEES

At the height of their fame, the Monkees were the most popular pop band on the planet. After beginning life as a group of actors, they eventually became a fully fledged pop band that recorded songs and performed concerts. To date, they've sold 65 million records.

GIRLS AND BOYS

The 1960s was a golden age for pop music. It was also a golden age for the star-makers – the managers, songwriters and music producers who worked away behind the scenes to turn bands and singers into stars.

Shining stars

In the 1960s, pop groups were much more popular than singers. Being in a pop group was not a guarantee of success, though. To become stars, you needed a good manager and a record producer who would make your songs sound good.

BEATLES MANAGER BRIAN EPSTEIN (LEFT) WAS ONE OF A NEW BREED OF BUSINESSPEOPLE WHO UNDERSTOOD HOW TO MAKE MONEY OUT OF POP MUSIC.

TOP MANAGER

The most successful pop manager of all was Brian Epstein, the man who turned the Beatles into the biggest band on the planet. Epstein knew that the Beatles sounded good, but to succeed they'd also need to look good on TV, too.

The importance of image

Epstein and other 1960s pop managers understood that 'image', or how a band looked, was an important part of their appeal to teenagers. Because of this, managers concentrated just as much on how a band looked as how they sounded.

Let's go surfing

The Beach Boys, one of the most popular groups of the 1960s, took pride in their appearance. Their smart-casual look matched their songs, which were mostly about girls, cars and surfing. Their all-American sound and look appealed to their teenage audience.

Motown sound

To help them sound good, 1960s pop groups worked with the best record producers. Norman Whitfield and Berry Gordy Junior, the men behind the Motown record label, understood this more than most. Between them, they produced hundreds of hit singles, almost single-handedly turning pop fans on to soul music.

INSIDE THE SOUND

BEAT MUSIC

The most popular form of pop music in the early 1960s was 'beat music', a British sound made popular by groups such as the Beatles. Based around a steady beat, its catchy songs combined rock and roll guitars with pop singing styles, sometimes influenced by American soul.

HITSVILLE USA IN DETROIT, THE ORIGINAL HOME OF SOUL RECORD LABEL MOTOWN, IS NOW A POPULAR MUSEUM.

FORMER SONG WRITER BERRY GORDY JUNIOR UNDERSTOOD HOW TO MAKE POP RECORDS, AND TURNED HIS COMPANY, MOTOWN RECORDS, INTO A HUGE BUSINESS EMPIRE.

The hit factory

Motown was one of the first pop 'hit factories' around. The company used the same musicians and producers to record songs with different singers, guaranteeing a consistent 'sound'. Today, hit factories are still an essential part of the pop music scene.

POP ART

By the mid-1960s pop music was growing up. While the charts were still full of short, catchy songs, many pop groups and singers had a desire to make more substantial music. Pop was becoming art.

Battle of the bands

Two of the world's biggest pop bands, the Beatles and the Beach Boys, led this change. Both groups were interested in other styles of music and wanted to include new sounds in their songs. So, they set about trying to reflect all of these influences in their music.

WITH THEIR *PET SOUNDS* ALBUM, THE BEACH BOYS TURNED THEIR BACK ON SURFING-INSPIRED POP IN FAVOUR OF SONGS THAT WERE MUCH MORE MUSICALLY COMPLEX.

Studio time

By 1966, the Beatles had decided to stop playing concerts. Instead, they spent more time at Abbey Road recording studios with record producer George Martin. They wanted to create a pop album that featured songs in many different styles, from folk-rock and Motown-style soul to tracks influenced by experimental classical music composers.

LANDMARK ALBUM

When it was released in 1966, the Beatles' *Revolver* album was hailed as a masterpiece. It didn't sound like any other pop album that had been made before. It used Indian instruments, soul-style horns, backwards guitar solos and special effects to enhance the sound.

Beat it

Revolver wasn't the only landmark album released in 1966. The Beach Boys' *Pet Sounds* set new standards for how pop albums were recorded, and was every bit as adventurous as *Revolver*. It's still thought of as one of the best albums of all time.

Classic pop

In 1967, the Beatles raised the bar again with their most famous album, *Sgt Pepper's Lonely Hearts Club Band*. Recorded over six months in Abbey Road, *Sgt Pepper* was the most inventive pop album ever made. Like *Pet Sounds*, it used sounds that had never been heard before on pop records – a full orchestra, inventive recording techniques and even fairground organs.

PAUL McCARTNEY ON THE BEACH BOYS

'*Pet Sounds* by the Beach Boys blew me out of the water. It might be going overboard to say it's a classic of the twentieth century, but to me it's almost unbeatable.'

Paul McCartney (pictured)

Art attack

Sgt Pepper and *Pet Sounds* started a trend for recording musically more interesting pop albums. They also proved, once and for all, that pop music could be about much more than just simple, radio-friendly songs.

BY TURNING THEIR BACK ON PLAYING LIVE TO SPEND MORE TIME IN THE RECORDING STUDIO, THE BEATLES CHANGED THE FACE OF POP MUSIC FOREVER.

THE AGE OF GLAMOUR

As the 1960s turned to the 1970s, the pop art of the Beach Boys and the Beatles was replaced by new pop music trends. With many older pop bands now making rock records, new pop stars emerged to entertain teenagers.

Glam it up

During the 1970s, the pop charts were dominated by a handful of new musical styles inspired by very different music. There was glam rock, a stomping new fusion of rock and pop, and disco, a style that emerged from the nightclubs of America to take the world by storm.

Family affair

Groups made up of family members were also popular. The Osmonds, Carpenters, Bee Gees and the Nolans were all made up of brothers and sisters. All were hugely successful, dominating the pop charts on both sides of the Atlantic.

THE OSMONDS WERE A FAMILY OF PERFORMERS FROM OGDEN, UTAH. THEY WERE ONE OF THE MOST POPULAR BANDS OF THE 1970S.

BROTHER-AND-SISTER ACT THE CARPENTERS WERE ONE OF THE MOST-PLAYED POP ACTS ON AMERICAN RADIO IN THE 1970S.

PLAYLIST

1970s POP

The Osmonds – *Crazy Horses* (1972)
Bay City Rollers – *Shang-A-Lang* (1974)
Bee Gees – *Nights on Broadway* (1975)
The Jackson 5 – *Blame it on the Boogie* (1978)
The Nolans – *I'm in the Mood for Dancing* (1979)

Fast forward

Pop music has always reflected musical trends, so it wasn't long before disco dominated the pop charts. For the first time, dance music was leading pop forwards into a new age.

WE ARE FAMILY

Another family group that enjoyed huge success in the 1970s was the Jackson 5. Signed to pop hit factory Motown, the five brothers made fun, feel-good soul music that people could dance to. As the 1970s progressed, they helped introduce disco to pop audiences.

DURING THE DISCO ERA IN THE LATE 1970S, THE JACKSON 5 ENJOYED MORE NUMBER ONE HITS THAN ANY OTHER SOUL BAND.

Dance to the music

Disco was an energetic, nightclub-friendly version of soul that had started life in the underground clubs of New York. As nightclubs began to spread around the world in the mid 1970s, dancing to disco records became wildly popular.

THE SYNTH-POP SCENE

By the early 1980s, disco had died and glam rock was a distant memory. In place of both came another style of popular music originally inspired by dance music culture, synth-pop.

Start the dance

As the 1970s turned to the 1980s, dance music producers began using new, cutting-edge electronic instruments such as synthesiser keyboards and drum machines. These allowed musicians and producers to create sounds and dance tracks that sounded futuristic.

Industrial roots

Pop music created using synthesisers first emerged from European cities such as Dusseldorf and Sheffield in the mid-1970s. To begin with, though, it was largely made by experimental acts with an interest in the potential of cutting-edge technology. By the early 1980s, though, synthesiser use was much more widespread and synth-pop was quickly gaining in popularity.

STEEL CITY

Sheffield, an industrial city in the north of England, was home to many of the synth-pop scene's leading acts. The Human League, Heaven 17 and ABC all enjoyed great success in the pop charts during the early part of the 1980s, having originally started out making experimental electronic music.

ABC WERE ONE OF A NUMBER OF SUCCESSFUL SYNTH-POP BANDS TO EMERGE FROM THE NORTHERN ENGLISH CITY OF SHEFFIELD, WHICH WAS PREVIOUSLY FAMOUS FOR PRODUCING STEEL.

American scene

The American dance scene, previously the birthplace of disco, also had a huge influence on the synth-pop sound of the 1980s. Madonna, now one of the most successful pop singers of all time, got her break singing in underground dance clubs in New York. Synth-pop star Prince started out playing in underground soul and disco bands in his home city of Minneapolis.

Dance-pop

The sounds of underground American and European dance music also had an influence on two of the most successful British synth-pop acts of the 1980s, Wham! and Pet Shop Boys. Both worked with top US dance producers early in their career, gaining popularity in the clubs before breaking into the pop charts.

AMERICAN SOUL STAR PRINCE TURNED TO SYNTH-POP IN THE 1980S AND BECAME ONE OF THE MOST RECOGNISABLE SINGERS ON THE PLANET.

LIVING LEGENDS

PET SHOP BOYS

Formed in 1984 in London by former pop journalist Neil Tennant and architecture student Chris Lowe, Pet Shop Boys are the most successful pop duo of all time. Famed for their love of outrageous costumes, they have sold over 50 million records worldwide since 1985.

VIDEO KILLED THE RADIO STAR

In the 1960s and 1970s, TV had the power to make or break pop careers thanks to shows such as *American Bandstand*. In the 1980s, the relationship continued to blossom. The era of music television had arrived.

I want my MTV

In 1981, some TV executives in upstate New York decided to launch a new cable TV station called MTV. Based around the idea of playing non-stop music videos, it would quickly go on to be the world's first 24-hour music TV station. It would also change pop music forever.

THE VIDEO AGE

Music videos were not a new concept. As far back as the 1960s popular bands such as the Beatles would record short films to promote their songs. By 1981, more and more pop acts were recording music videos.

Right place, right time

MTV came at the right time. The first music video shown by the station, *Video Killed the Radio Star* by British act Buggles, perfectly summed up the mood of the time. Music videos were now the most important tool for promoting pop acts around

KING OF POP MICHAEL JACKSON STARTED THE TREND FOR SPENDING HUGE AMOUNTS OF MONEY MAKING MUSIC VIDEOS, WITH AN EXTENDED FILM FOR HIS SONG *THRILLER*.

the world.

Pop TV

MTV was almost an overnight success. Teenagers, the core market for pop groups, would spend hours every day watching a constant stream of brand new music videos. To stand out from the crowd, it was vital for pop groups to make ever more elaborate and expensive videos.

Trendsetters

The two biggest pop stars of the 1980s, Madonna and Michael Jackson, embraced this change. Their record labels spent huge amounts of money making their videos, in the hope that they would create a stir. Jackson's *Thriller* video, which featured him dancing with a troupe of zombies, cost an astonishing $500,000.

BIG BUDGETS

Thirty years later, record labels still spend huge amounts of money creating stunning music videos for their biggest pop acts. The promotional clip for Madonna's 2012 song *Give Me All Your Loving* cost a cool $1.5 million.

RIHANNA ON MADONNA

'Madonna is a great inspiration. She has reinvented her clothing style and music with success so many times, remaining a real force in entertainment.'

Rihanna (pictured)

MADONNA WORKED WITH TOP FASHION DESIGNERS TO MAKE SURE THAT SHE HAD AN EXCITING NEW LOOK FOR EACH MUSIC VIDEO SHE MADE.

19

WHEN WILL I BE FAMOUS?

The dawn of 24-hour music television didn't just make stars of synth-pop acts with an eye for fashionable clothes. It also saw the return of 'manufactured' pop groups put together by ambitious managers.

Mixed audience

Although synth-pop stars such as Madonna and Michael Jackson appealed to teenagers, they also had older followers. The same couldn't be said for many of the manufactured acts of the late '80s and early '90s. These good-looking young men and women were chosen by their managers to appeal to teenagers.

MADONNA CONTINUED TO ENJOY SUCCESS IN THE MANUFACTURED POP ERA, THANKS TO HER ABILITY TO TRANSFORM HER LOOK AND SOUND.

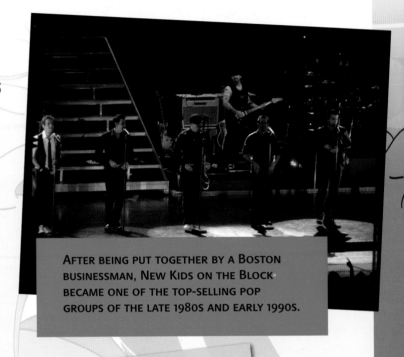

AFTER BEING PUT TOGETHER BY A BOSTON BUSINESSMAN, NEW KIDS ON THE BLOCK BECAME ONE OF THE TOP-SELLING POP GROUPS OF THE LATE 1980S AND EARLY 1990S.

BOY BANDS

Amongst the most manufactured acts of the time were Bros, a trio that featured identical twins Luke and Matt Goss, and New Kids on the Block. The latter, formed in 1985 by record producer Maurice Starr, were the biggest 'boy band' of the 1980s.

Hangin' tough

New Kids on the Block was phenomenally successful. After earning their first record contract in 1986, the five schoolfriends from Boston went on to dominate the pop charts. They split up in 1994 after selling over 80 million records worldwide.

HIT FACTORY

Over in the UK, a trio of record producers had set their sights on setting up their own hit factory. Mike Stock, Matt Aitken and Pete Waterman were the 1980s version of the Motown businessmen of the 1960s.

Puppet masters

Stock, Aitken and Waterman became famous for finding fresh talent and producing huge chart hits. They understood pop music and the importance of television as a promotional tool. They even signed actors from popular TV soap operas, such as Kylie Minogue and Jason Donovan, and turned them into pop stars.

Many hits

Until their decline in the 1990s, Stock, Aitken and Waterman produced over 100 UK top 40 hits, many of which were also big in America. Between them, the trio worked with many successful bands and singers such as Bananarama, Dead or Alive, LaToyah Jackson, Mel & Kim and Brother Beyond.

BRITISH GIRL GROUP BANANARAMA WERE ONE OF THE MOST SUCCESSFUL ACTS PRODUCED BY HIT-MAKERS STOCK, AITKEN AND WATERMAN.

THE PUPPET MASTERS

The success of manufactured pop acts such as Bros and New Kids on the Block between 1988 and 1993 inspired many keen businessmen to create their own pop groups. The manager was once again the most important person in pop.

Manufactured stars

The 1990s and 2000s were a golden age for manufactured pop groups. In Europe, in particular, there was little stopping the success of acts such as Boyzone, Westlife, Take That and the Spice Girls. Behind each manufactured group was a manager pulling the strings.

Puppet on a string

Most manufactured groups have little say in the songs they play or the clothes they wear. Their manager arranges all this for them. If they are a success, they will become millionaires, as will the manager.

SCOOTER BRAUN MANAGED JUSTIN BIEBER TO INTERNATIONAL SUPERSTARDOM AFTER SPOTTING HIM PERFORMING ON YOUTUBE WHEN BIEBER WAS JUST 13 YEARS OLD.

BAND BASICS

The idea behind manufactured pop groups is simple. A manager holds an audition, where interested singers get a chance to impress them. After that, a handful of people get picked to be in 'the group', and the search for a record deal begins.

IRISH SUCCESS

Another wildly successful manager was Louis Walsh, an Irishman who decided to put together an Irish rival to Take That. Boyzone and Westlife, the two bands he managed, were a runaway success.

Music moguls

The 1990s saw the rise of a number of powerful pop managers. Take That, the most successful British boy band of all time, were managed by a former TV casting agent called Nigel Martin-Smith.

Spice up your life

The most successful pop manager of the age, though, was Simon Fuller. The man behind the biggest girl group of the era, the Spice Girls, Fuller built his pop management business into a thriving global empire. Over the years, his acts have notched up 500 number one pop hits around the world.

LIVING LEGENDS

THE SPICE GIRLS

In the late 1990s, the world fell in love with five outspoken British girls and their fun brand of pop music. Their 'girl power' message proved so popular with fans that they starred in their own movie, *Spice World*, in 1997. In 2012, they reunited to appear at the closing ceremony of the London Olympics.

IT'S TALENT THAT MATTERS

After dominating the music charts in the 1990s, pop manager Simon Fuller decided to start making TV programmes. The shows he came up with revolutionised the relationship between pop and TV.

S Club 7

Fuller's first attempt to take pop to TV was a Monkees-like show about a teen band called *S Club 7*. It was a modest success, being shown in 100 different countries around the world.

Talent shows reinvented

Fuller's next idea was simple. He would reinvent an old classic TV format from the past, the talent show. A popular style of programme during the 1970s, talent shows allowed ordinary people to showcase their talents – be it singing, dancing or telling jokes – and win prizes.

POP MANAGER TURNED TV PRODUCER SIMON FULLER WAS GIVEN A STAR ON THE HOLLYWOOD WALK OF FAME IN 2011 IN RECOGNITION OF HIS CONTRIBUTION TO THE ENTERTAINMENT INDUSTRY.

POP IDOL

Fuller's show, *Pop Idol*, was to be different to '70s talent shows. It would offer contestants the chance to win a record deal and a contract with his management agency. Fuller and fellow pop manager Simon Cowell would reap the rewards when the winner's single rocketed to number one.

Reality bites

Pop Idol launched on British TV in October 2001. It featured a panel of expert judges, including Cowell and pop record producer Pete Waterman. It was a runaway success and helped launch the career of winner Will Young.

SIMON COWELL

Although now known for his TV talent shows, Simon Cowell first made his name in the pop music industry. He worked his way up from the mailroom of major label EMI to become a top executive at BMG Records. During that time, he also managed a number of pop acts, including successful 1980s singer Sinitta.

American idols

It was in America, though, that Fuller and Cowell's show would become most famous. Re-made as *American Idol* by Fox, it became a ratings smash and helped turn winners, such as Kelly Clarkson, into massive stars.

Huge success

Fuller and Cowell followed up the Idol series with a number of other TV talent shows, such as *X Factor* and *America's Got Talent*. Ten years on, reality TV talent shows are as popular as ever. Fuller and Cowell are now among the most powerful men in the entertainment industry.

KELLY CLARKSON SHOT TO FAME AFTER WINNING THE FIRST *AMERICAN IDOL* COMPETITION IN 2002.

URBAN ALL STARS

While Simon Fuller and Simon Cowell's pop TV talent shows were creating stars, another shift was taking place in pop music. For the first time, two previously underground styles of urban music were dominating the pop charts.

Old styles, new sound

By the time they began to become wildly popular in the early 2000s, hip-hop and R&B were already well-established styles of music. Both have their roots in the underground American black music scene that had once given the world soul and disco.

SINCE FIRST GRACING THE POP CHARTS IN THE 1990S, USHER HAS BECOME THE WORLD'S MOST POPULAR R&B SINGER, AND TO DATE HAS SOLD OVER 65 MILLION RECORDS.

Black beats

Over the years, most styles of pop music have in some way grown out of black music culture. Rock and roll, disco, dance music and even synth-pop can trace their roots back to styles of music invented by black Americans. For the most part, though, the styles have been altered to suit white audiences.

SINGER FAITH EVANS IS ONE OF A NEW BREED OF SOUL SINGERS TO ENJOY INTERNATIONAL POP SUCCESS ON THE BACK OF R&B SONGS.

Swing thing

Hip-hop and R&B were different. For starters, the majority of the scene's stars were black Americans themselves. There was also no need to soften the sound or use white singers, as both black and white teenagers absolutely loved the music.

INSIDE **THE SOUND**

R&B

R&B as we know it today differs from traditional pop music in many ways. Firstly, it uses loose beats borrowed from hip-hop (as opposed to the rigid beat patterns of dance or synth-pop). It also emphasises the importance of heavy basslines and usually features soulful male or female vocals.

HIP-POP

The first hint of these two urban styles taking over the charts came in 1990, when girl groups TLC and Destiny's Child became huge stars as a result of a sound that mixed R&B and pop. Some time in the early 2000s the dam burst, and suddenly hip-hop and R&B acts were the biggest pop stars in the world.

RAPPER TURNED BUSINESSMAN SEAN 'P DIDDY' COMBS HELPED MAKE HIP-HOP AND R&B THE MOST POPULAR STYLES OF POP MUSIC AROUND IN THE LATE 1990S AND EARLY 2000S.

Global sound

Former Destiny's Child singer Beyoncé was the first to climb to the top of the pop music tree, closely followed by Usher, Missy Elliot, Faith Evans, Jay-Z and P Diddy. Since then, many other acts have followed in their footsteps. Even traditional pop singers, such as Madonna and Mariah Carey, have embraced the urban sound of R&B.

TALK ABOUT POP MUSIC

In the twenty-first century, pop music is just as vital and exciting as it has ever been. It continues to react to technological changes and to draw on fresh new influences from other genres. Who knows where it will take us next?

Music on the move

The Internet has had a huge impact on all areas of our lives, but none more so than the way we access music. Thanks to smartphones, tablet computers and video sharing sites such as YouTube, we can watch and listen to fresh new pop music whenever we want.

Video stars

Although the way we access music videos has changed, they're still hugely popular. Record companies still spend huge amounts of money on creating top quality videos, and managers still want their pop groups to appear on popular TV shows.

DOWNLOAD REVOLUTION

The Internet has changed the way we buy music. The days of the 7-inch single, once a staple of pop music, are long gone. Now, we can buy our favourite pop tracks at the push of a button, through online website and music stores.

RUSSIAN POP SINGER ELKA IS A HUGE STAR IN HER OWN COUNTRY. POP MUSIC IS NOW A TRULY GLOBAL MOVEMENT.

Changes

Pop music itself continues to evolve, too, but often looks to the past. In recent years, top pop stars have enjoyed hits with tracks that sound like '80s synth-pop, Motown soul and classic dance music. Even R&B stars such as Rihanna and Beyoncé are making dance-pop records.

Global pop

The biggest change in the last 50 years has been the spread of pop music worldwide. What started out as a variant of underground black American music in the 1950s has been adopted and adapted by musicians all over the world.

Same but different

Wherever you go in the world, you will find pop music. From South Korea to South America, traditional global musical styles are being mixed with American pop or European dance to create thrilling new fusions. Pop is now a genuine global artform.

BLACK EYED PEAS STARTED LIFE AS AN UNDERGROUND HIP-HOP CREW, BEFORE STORMING UP THE CHARTS WITH A STRING OF POP-DANCE HITS.

KOREAN ARTIST PSY'S *GANGNAM STYLE* MUSIC VIDEO WAS A HUGE HIT ON YOUTUBE, AND TO DATE HAS BEEN WATCHED NEARLY 900 MILLION TIMES.

GLOSSARY

Album A collection of songs.

Artform A type of art, for example music, painting or acting.

Distinctive Unusual and easily recognised.

Drum machine A piece of equipment used by dance and pop artists to create beats and drum patterns.

Evolve To change over time.

Executive Someone high up in a company, for example a director or senior manager.

Experimental Music or other art that is born out of trying different or unusual things.

Fusion Mixing together two or more different musical styles.

Gramophone A piece of equipment used to listen to records.

Groundbreaking Important and historic.

Manufactured pop A style of pop music created by managers and record labels, featuring singers and dancers who have been hand picked to appeal to teenagers.

Masterpiece A great work of art, be it music, painting or sculpture.

Nightclub A place where people go to dance to loud music.

Notched up Achieved.

Pop A form of upbeat mainstream music. This word is short for 'popular'.

Record A pressed plastic disc featuring recorded music. The forerunner of the CD.

Record label A company that specialises in recording and selling pop music.

Record producer Someone who specialises in recording songs and making them sound as good as possible.

Recording studio The rooms or building used to record and produce music.

Revolution An important event or series of events that changes the course of history.

Single A musical release featuring one or two pop songs. It can be a record, CD or digital download.

Synthesiser An electronic instrument that looks like a small piano.

Thriving Successful.

TV format A style of TV programme, for example a quiz show or soap opera.

Underground Not popular and well-known – usually of interest to serious fans only.

Vital Lively and important.

FURTHER INFORMATION

Further Reading

From Abba to Zoom: A Pop Culture Encyclopedia of the Late 20th Century by David Mansour (Andrews McMeel Publishing, 2005)

The History of American Pop by Stuart A Kallen (Lucent Books, 2012)

The History of Modern Music by Matt Anniss (Franklin Watts, 2012)

History of Motown by Virginia Aronson (Chelsea House Publishers, 2002)

Sound Trackers: 1980s Pop by Bob Brunning (Heinemann, 1999)

Websites

www.billboard.com/charts/hot-100
Find out what's topping the US pop charts this week. The site also contains loads of great facts and figures about previous US chart-toppers.

www.factmonster.com/ipka/ A0885982.html
All you need to know about 250 years of American popular music history, in one easy timeline.

www.guardian.co.uk/music/2004/ may/02/popandrock/
British newspaper the Guardian offers a run down of some of the most important moments in the history of pop music. An excellent history lesson!

www.rollingstone.com/music/lists/ the-500-greatest-songs-of-all- time-20110407
The stories behind the 500 greatest pop and rock songs of all time, picked by America's leading music magazine, Rolling Stone.

www.youtube.com/music/pop
Watch the latest music videos and classic clips from years gone by.

INDEX

SERIES CONTENTS

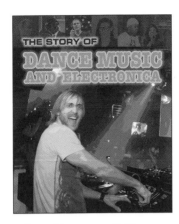

The Story of Dance Music and Electronica

The Dawn of the DJ • The Synthesiser Revolution • Let There be House • Into the Future • This is Acid • Hardcore Uproar • Chill Out • Going Live • Superstar DJs, Here We Go! • Panic at the Disco! • Bass, How Low Can You Go? • Heroes of the Pop Charts • Dance Planet

The Story of Hip-Hop

Block Party Roots • Rapper's Delight • Scratchin' that Itch • Walk this Way • Fight the Power • Hardcore Hip-House • East Coast Vs West Coast • Flower Power • Don't Forget about Dre • Big Business • Talk about Pop Music • Pushing Boundaries • Hip-Hop Planet

The Story of Pop Music

The Pre-History of Pop • Rock Around the Clock • On the Box • Girls and Boys • Pop Art • The Age of Glamour • The Synth-Pop Scene • Video Killed the Radio Star • When Will I be Famous? • The Puppet Masters • It's Talent that Matters • Urban All Stars • Talk About Pop Music

The Story of Punk and Indie

Downtown Revolution • Anarchy in the UK • Do It Yourself • Post-Punk • Indie-Pop and Gothic Rock • The Birth of Alternative Rock • Start the Dance • Alternative Goes Mainstream • The Birth of Britpop • Stadium Punk • What Goes Around, Comes Around • When I Ruled the World • Evolving Sounds

The Story of Rock Music

Blues Roots • Rock and Roll Revolution • The British Invasion • Open Your Mind • Living for the Weekend • Glam It Up • Progress • Getting Heavy • Stadium Rock! • Alternative Rock • Changing of the Guard • Looking Back to Look Forward • It's All Rock

The Story of Soul and R&B

The Roots of Soul • The First Soul Stars • The Hit Factory • Funk Brothers and Soul Sisters • Making a Point • The Sound of Philadelphia • You Should be Dancing • Rip It Up and Start Again • Blue-Eyed Soul • Swing Thing • Brand Neo • R&B Goes Global • Big Business

ARABIAN DAYS

ARABIAN DAYS
EDNA O'BRIEN

PHOTOGRAPHS BY GERARD KLIJN

QUARTET BOOKS
LONDON MELBOURNE NEW YORK

First published in 1977 by Quartet Books Limited
a member of the Namara Group
27 Goodge Street, London W1P 1FD

Copyright © 1977 by Edna O'Brien

Gérard Klijn's photographs
by arrangement with Heinrich Hanau Publications

Photograph of His Highness Sheikh Zayed bin Sultan
Al-Nahyan by Dick Dawson
and reproduced by courtesy of London Weekend Television

ISBN 0 7043 2150 5

Design by Mike Jarvis

Printed in Great Britain by
Acorn Litho Feltham Middx.
and bound by Mansell Limited, Witham, Essex

'Oh how shall I tear the East out of my heart?'

So said Lady Isabel Burton, the exemplary wife of Sir Richard Burton, as she left Damascus in 1871 soon after her husband had been dismissed from his post in the Consulate. She was seen off at dawn by her friend Lady Jane Digby, an Englishwoman who in middle years had flung herself headlong into the East and married a Bedouin chief. It is said that Lady Jane delighted in the nomadic life and in the wild gallop of the horsemen as they played with their lances, fired their pistols and threw themselves like schoolboys under the horses' bellies. She too threw herself into their world that was spare, harsh and exigent. Yet in some way it was fascinating. As with Karen Blixen in Kenya, she became the tribe's adviser on farming, medicine, education and domestic quarrels. She has not left us an immemorial work such as *Out of Africa*, but nevertheless she set an example to imprudent English-women who would quit the domestic hearth. She rode to warfare with blackened eyes and a dagger, a woman devoid of fright. The desert, the people and a turbulent romantic love gave her a new lease of life. The question is, would it now? I have my doubts.

The world is not the dashing place it once seemed and modern adventurers require not so much courage, incentive and individuality as patience, money, ear-plugs and a sense of humour. But one thing is still true, distant travel is a radical thing. It leads to undiscovered zones within and without. Not always do we fall in love, sometimes we recoil, or give expression to hidden emotions – rage, fear and an exasperation at finding everything different, being at odds with our faithfully cherished habits and ideas. At least we get a spur on. We ask what their government is like, how do they vote – that is if they do vote – how pervasive is their religion, how circumscribed their sex, what their moods, their dress, their food, are they open or are they mistrustful, can one absorb or be absorbed by them? Love thy neighbour as thyself. It is an impossible precept.

I am thinking now of the East. The East where Holman Hunt travelled for two years sketching the faces that resembled the face of Christ. Arabia, where Mr Robin Bidwell in his book *Travellers in Arabia* says more people have gone to discover themselves rather than the peninsula. He was referring mostly to the Victorian age when travellers wearied of the stilted, circumscribed life of England and went where their imaginations as well as their minds and bodies would be given rein and vigour. It is not the same today, having jumped from its poor relatively empty untouched state to a society that is industrial, yet has not undergone an industrial revolution. A land of Babel.

Last year I had a short stay in the Middle East. I met – as I had not met in England – people from every walk of life. Sheikh Zayed bin Sultan al-Nahyan, the Ruler of Abu Dhabi, his favourite wife Sheikha Fatima, the Foreign Minister Mr Ahmad Suweidi, Iranians, Iraqis, Indians, Jordanians, numerous hairdressers, rich families and poor, a secret poetess, transplanted Bedouins, hawks, camels and a fairly consistent sunshine. I have a picture of them in my mind that perhaps is not one they will recognize readily. Their utopian dreams may perhaps clash with mine. I believe that we ought to nourish each other's imagination but a new country has the tremendous indefatigable task of

building itself from scratch. The costly and euphemistic brochure kit that I was given was in blue and silver, the very colours of moonlight. It had as its heraldic motif the phrase – 'Where dreams come true.' Traffic expansion, foreign policy, welfare, child and adult education, making the desert bloom – these as its themes. At least the desert was there, the flaming wilderness that one had read and reread of – the desert, interminable, empty, with sloughs of mud, lagoons of salt; the desert wavy and opal, with the hot harsh wind, so hot and so harsh that the travellers had to be wrapped in cloaks which covered their faces as well as their bodies, and that even the camels, those living epitomes of endurance, sometimes were not able to endure. An Englishman, Mr R. A. Hamilton, said with true clairvoyance to those who might go to the desert that, 'Not a day will pass in all your life but you will remember some facet of that opal land, not a night will pass without some twist of dream.'

Once upon a time the desert, still the desert, and now city, instant city at that.

The images cede, recede, because there is so much. Faces of the East, skins like prunes, like peonies; hooded hawks, hooded women. The spires of concrete towering up. Such audacious monstrosities. The mosques' roundness, like basins of white. Inside the praying, stooping, supplicating men – O Allah the Almighty, the All-Merciful. A little file of trees starved for rain. The water merely lodges in the air, the humidity catching the breath and making crinkles of one's hair. In the desert beyond are the blazing torches of flame, the burning bushes, the pillars of fire such as we Christians were forewarned of for the last day. Some women wear capacious dresses, bright blue chiffon with crusts of stars affixed. The workers in the backs of lorries are piled in; their headgear more significant, more noticeable, more telling than their very faces. Coils of

baked cloth. A man is what? His genitals? His wives? His mind? His money? A man is what? The city pulsates under the din of cranes, drills and motor cars. The wayside is a shock of sand, white, merciless, unpretty. There is no romance here, how could there be? The air murmurs with money. A bright glaze hovers and simmers across the city. A bird of passage, I wait, I wait.

Such were my first jumbled impressions of the city of Abu Dhabi and my first experience of the East. I had gone with many illusions, a compendium based on the notions and excitements of other travellers, very often male travellers, who braved the harsh and toilsome plateaus and through their journeys transformed themselves, and triumphed over impossible circumstances. Such a one in the 1870s was Mr Charles Doughty, a man of lofty and sable disposition. He had taken on his travels £12 in gold, a thermometer and a revolver. He stayed for two years, travelling more or less like a beggar. An English lady called Mrs Mabel Bent in the 1890s made her journey in style, bringing her own husband, her own botanist, numerous servants and a naturalist. Mr Wilfred Thesiger in the years immediately after the Second World War brought a camera, an aneroid, a press for plants, a small medicine chest, a volume of Gibbon and a copy of *War and Peace*. I brought Mr Thesiger, Mr Doughty, Mr Burckhardt, Miss Sybille Bedford, the *I-Ching*, Collis Browne's Chlorodyne and a supply of white wine since I feared it might be unavailable. I was wrong. It was available but a half-bottle of French white wine cost the exalted sum of £5.

There, everything is imported – long sheep from Romania, beef from Australia, fruit, vegetables and some of the couture from Lebanon, fine furniture from Italy, scooters, transistors and televisions from Japan, cars, machinery, stainless steel, aluminium and kerbing from England and France, wood from Norway and Sweden,

HIS HIGHNESS SHEIKH ZAYED BIN SULTAN AL-NAHYAN PRESIDENT OF
THE UNITED ARAB EMIRATES AND RULER OF ABU DHABI

CAVITY
C25

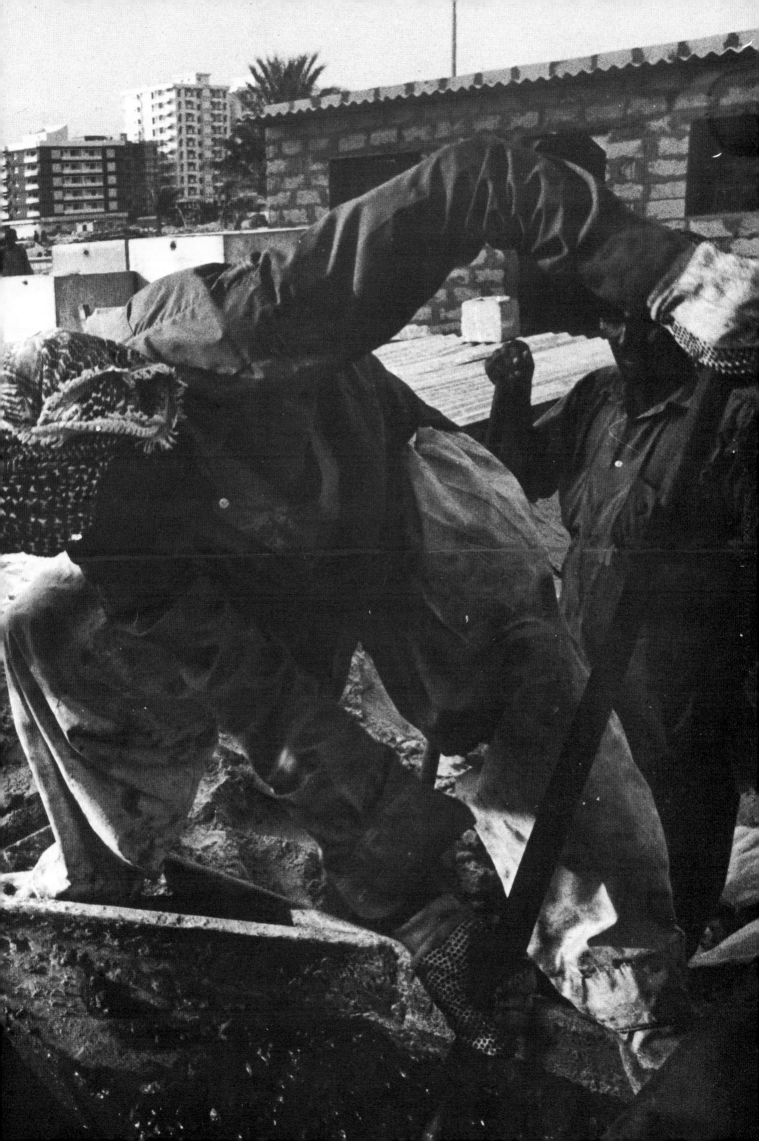

grass from Mexico. Everything except for the magic oil with which to my surprise and for want of more aesthetic things I became acquainted.

The incongruities are immense. From outside, an apartment dwelling might look like a building site, yet inside a salon reveals treasures in glass cases, redolent of the *Arabian Nights*. Here the rubies and the necklaces, gold leaf, ivory, exotica. Here as well the bric-à-brac from the West, gilt ornaments, china camels, a candle with 'London' stippled into the wax.

It is another culture or semi-culture. I felt I was among people of changing consciousness that had not yet reached a fundamental identity.

Abu Dhabi had taken a plunge into the twentieth century but how was I to know that? I had not imagined towers of concrete as far as the eye could see, cranes, tanks, a sense of unfinishedness as if the place had just been dropped higgledy-piggledy from the sky.

In a way the city's rise is like that of a film star. A backwater until the late 1950s, a forgotten place, largely desert with two oases and a village, no more than a settlement of dwellings made of palm fronds, and a fortress that was its palace. They had lived on pearl fishing, on dates and on the milk from their camels when their camels were not carrying. Camel milk is said to be purgative. To them pasture was a few sparse areas of herb and dried thorn-bush on which the ever-resourceful camel grazed. What the then ruler Sheikh Shakhbut ordered the drilling for, was not oil but water. The first oil shaft was sunk in 1956 and a few years later they discovered wells both offshore and onshore deep down under the dunes. The prodigal riches began in the 1970s. Now a country with the largest per capita income in the world, Abu Dhabi's is like the story of Cinderella whom I met after the ball in the early discomfiting hours of dawn.

It is in many senses a new country although it must be true to say of it as Yeats said of Petra that it is half as old as time. Yeats would not like it. It is raw, tough, patriarchal, enthusiastic, busy, righteous, puzzling, unhaunted and powerful. It is a country whose bloodstream issues money. A fairy godmother to her own and to others. Business booms. Agencies boom. Contracts boom. Trade missions are as numerous and as important as once the caravan missions to Mecca. The expatriates grow rich. Their leisure life is not particularly enviable. The working bachelors, the men in oil, the men in drilling, the technicians, the agronomists, are very short of women. The local women are reticent and guarded in the extreme. There is no theatre, no art gallery and the bookshop gave as much pride of place to crockery as to literature. It is not for the mandarins!

Its Ruler, Shiekh Zayed, seems to inspire much love and awe. He is a striking man. His looks are phenomenal. Looking at the photos of him I could not but think of a namesake of his that Mr Doughty had singled out: 'One of hollow cheeks with eyes that looked austerely on a lawless land of famine where his nourishment was coffee and tobacco and his virtue a courageous forbearing and an abiding of hunger.'

He has no visible truck with age, shows no flab and no physical dissolution. His body and bearing bespeak a man who did not get rich too soon. Sufficiently weathered in the ways of hardship, he does not seem to be destroyed or softened by the wealth oil has brought him and his country. According to his people he is in touch with every aspect and every need of their lives.

Of course I wanted to meet him. Who would not?

It was the first thing on my list on that first morning, dazed from heat, bewildered by the inevitable jet-lag when I went to the Ministry office. It was a new office and in my honour were a covey of men. One of them wel-

comed me very formally, as an individual, as a writer and as an emissary of my country. They all shook hands with me. Hovering around the door were the young boys, stationed there to open it, or to close it, or to provide coffee. At once I was to learn the coffee ritual. The young boy (a Pakistani or an Indian) would bring it in an ornate silver pot with a beak-like spout and pass each person a little china cup that was like a doll's cup without handle. A mere dribble of coffee was poured in and one was to drink it straight away. It had an unfamiliar smell. I asked what it was and after much to-do we all learnt that it was carda-mom but none of us knew why it was put in coffee. Then I was told the gestures to make – if you required more coffee you just continued to hold the cup and it would be refilled automatically, but to show you had had enough you shook it round and round. Yes we were all smiling.

Sitting opposite in utmost and smouldering silence was a beautiful Bedouin gentleman who never raised his eyes. He, like many others, comes to any of these Ministry offices any morning, without appointment, and so the existing chaos gets added to. He seemed totally unper-turbed and I thought that perhaps when one is used to it the hot sun is a calming thing and takes the fret out of one. It was there that I fell in love with the male Arab attire. Some of the men in the Ministry were dressed in dark suits and ties but some had clung to their original garb and this had all the sanctity of an apostle's outfit. It was chastity incarnate – the long frock coat, the headpiece of soft, white, almost transparent cloth held down by two folds of elasticized black cording. This headgear, I soon saw, could be worn in so many ways so that with a mere tilt the wearer could seem chaste or jaunty or devilish or saintly or whatever.

Please, they were saying, what kind of book was I

writing? I said I would like to see the desert, see the tribes, see the Arabia that I had read of. Did I then see in their eyes the first flicker of rejection? The future, they said, was the thing to write about and not the past. There and then we made lists. They made lists and I made lists – a doctor, a lady doctor, a school-teacher, His Highness the Ruler, His Excellency the Foreign Minister and as many other people as possible. And a helicopter that would take me to Liwa where I would see the date palms in the heart of the desert. I would see the camels, the statuesque desert camels, and not the two-tired fawn beasts that I could see from the window of the office, in some allotment. I had lists for every hour of every day, but it was not to be like that. It was all to be much slower and more vexing and I would wait in my hotel for one or other of these appointments and I would take out a notebook and write one of these profound generalizations that mean or meant nothing at all.

I suppose I do not like improvisation. Nor was I prepared for a landscape where I would see simply ads and posters for formica-faced cubicles, hydraulic cranes, drilling buckets, diaphragm walls, roof treatment and prefabricated villas. I had come both too soon and too late.

There is an importance, and a frenzy that comes from being new and rich. Everyone is in a hurry. Husbands and even in some cases wives are busy getting on with the business of making their country prosper and cut a figure in the world. There is the same fervour that I perceived in Cuba in 1968 and the same commitment to the Ruler. Not of course the same politics, or the same poverty or the same deprivation. Here there is no hardship except that of climate and confusedness. There is no financial *angst*. No beggars as in Marrakesh, no maimed children as in India.

In short there is prosperity. But the texture of life is blurred as each person hurries to fulfil this mission of serving country. Conferences and conventions abound and no sooner have the important personages come back from one of these important assemblies than they are off to another while their assistants are already gone to pave the way, and lesser assistants are in unfinished government offices trying to cope with the unfamiliar and modern task of bureaucracy.

Very soon I felt homesick. The savage loves his native shore. The domestic life that I normally rail against, struck me as being dear and purposeful. I wanted a disguise, to wear Eastern clothing, to put henna on my hands and feet, and to pass as one of them. I wanted access. I wanted to understand. From my room I could see a variety of pale colours that called for as yet uncrystallized adjectives. Suffice it to say that the water was of the softest, lightest, merest blue, and on the near horizon the blue was so hazy that it was as if the lining had dropped out of the clouds. The air itself was full of nourishment before the sun came up.

No one ever talks of the weather, at least not in terms of what it does to one's humour and one's constitution. We say it's fine or it rained or it stormed or it snowed but we do not define its effect on us. I had read about the humidity but I did not know that even in February I would move about zestlessly, I would gasp and think of my own rainy refreshing country. They said I would get acclimatized to it. The word at last took on its true particularity for me. No progress. The woman in purdah, the Ruler out of the country, other officials delivering condolences (very long condolences) to India and the rest of the nation overworked. I had a little pen picture with which to comfort myself. A reclining female in a Rossetti setting, high green grass banks, river, a tangle of water lilies, dew and damp.

But then of course I had not yet seen the desert, not yet experienced that great sensation of light, space, immense solitude, and the fear or thrill of levitation. I had to wait. Things were being arranged. Everything moved slowly. I sat in my hotel room and read a book of proverbs – *Torches in the Darkness*, it said. I read at random:

'A butting ox is better than an empty bed' – Is it?
'The threshold weeps forty days when a girl is born' – Does it?
'When a woman goes on a journey it is because a man opens the door for her.'

The wireless and the papers were filled with events about roads, trade, a multi-million-pound sports complex, pollution and international cooperation. Queen Alia of Jordan had died and Arab womanhood had lost a champion. She was learning to fly. Other women, so the papers said, were on visits to Europe forging links with the wives of presidents and statesmen, meeting women in every walk of life! Doing the very thing I wanted to do! Brigitte Bardot and a galaxy of greats were expected for the opening of an exclusive club in Sharjah in the autumn. Ooh-la-la, the headlines said, and went on to say that the grass which was coming from Mexico could well revolutionize the gardens of the Gulf. But that was not till the autumn!

I would make phone calls to try and make appointments, or make phone calls to ask other people to try and make appointments or, as they so quaintly put it, 'to assist in the arranging of the making of appointments'. And there my troubles began. There were lots of reasons for this. Haste and blunder on the surface, and deep inside a resistance on their part to be seen – as if I had come to poach on their passions. They will smile at you at first,

but they will not trust you. So you ring again and you resay that you would like to see the Ruler, or the Ruler's wife, or the Ruler's son, or a school-teacher, or a lady gynaecologist, or a poet, or a lawyer, or an Indian magician, or whoever, and you are told that they too hope. *Inshallah*. The first word I learnt in Arabic, just as long ago in Spain, I learnt the refrain of 'tomorrow' – *mañana*. But 'I hope' does not mean tomorrow. In fact it has no guarantee at all, except that it is a nice expression. It is not just to a visitor that they say it but to each other. Desert hardship has bred a philosophy of uncertainty and they know that man is not governor of his own fate. He merely dangles the reins.

In the hotel lobby men would arrive, sit down, open their briefcases, while other men, their prospective buyers, would examine terms and tenders. The Arab men like gold, and not only wristwatches and bracelets caught the eye but always it seemed that some dark-haired hand was flicking on a gold lighter. Smoking was ubiquitous. I suppose it is a sign of liberty. Their voices and their appearance did not match. Their appearance was like that of acolytes, white, serene and religious, whereas their voices had a peep in the throat, and even that of the most masculine of men had a plangent note somewhere in its root. They talked rapidly. Very often when they met they greeted each other by touching noses. They did not seem to mind their surroundings. Perhaps pioneering people like an absence of class and absence of tradition, like things to be makeshift. In that way everyone's potential is the same.

As the days went on, I began to notice more of their character, how they were proud, how they were touchy, and how they had an irrational fear of being misunderstood. The reasons for this are so many. Theirs is like the fate of a film star who has been discovered, made famous, and is struggling for the first time with the different demands of fame, necessity and glamour. They are too busy. There is no cohesion, it is as if no one has consulted anybody else and no one has listened. The telephone lines are all busy. Those who worked in the offices were themselves amused as well as flabbergasted by the fact that they were in a turmoil and always waiting for a mechanic or a plasterer or a second persona to cope with the inundation.

Of course some had leisure. The elderly doctor who had been there for over twenty-five years sat surrounded by photos of himself from bygone days. There too his framed university degree and alongside it a glorious testimonial for services rendered signed by a number of sheikhs. He is on his first or second or third whisky. No patients have arrived yet. The room next door is a dispensary. He sits and gazes. His male Baluchi servant had gone for his evening prayer to the mosque. A shout precedes each massive call for whisky. Once he tells me he shouted so much that the air-conditioning plant fell from its socket and fortunately missed him. I asked about his practice and if the women use contraception. He says he would rather not reply to that, that I had better ask a woman doctor. But the woman doctor had declined to see me lest I unveil something that should not be exposed. All he will say is that they enjoy being given an injection. He tells me a little story. When he first came to those parts it was just dunes and a hut or two; a native woman came in with her husband for an injection and when, true to her innate modesty she refused to take off her underclothes, her husband just ripped them off her. He laughs. I laugh. He asks if I've been to the British Club. I recall the dark oak furniture and the company men treating themselves to gin and tonics as if it were Old England or perhaps one of Graham Greene's expatriate limbos, a territory of the mind.

In another room I talked to a Beluch woman as she sat on her unmade bed surrounded by children. One could hardly tell the difference in age between each of the

crawling infants. She and I made gestures. There was a stench of pee. In direct contrast to her surrounds she was wearing a vivid red gauze sari and a considerable consignment of gold. She did not know or want to know that there was a world outside. She would laugh or smile. Her mind seemed not to be ticking. She was without *angst*.

Another time I visited the fat merchant's wife. Ah yes, I still picture her sitting in her cool high-ceilinged parlour with plates of nougat and plates of cake for the early-morning visitors. Each morning her friends come and occasionally for the sake of one of the young girls a fortune-teller is called in. She is usually a Lebanese. The method of prediction is with ground coffee in the bottom of a cup and invariably the hoped-for prediction is marriage to a rich man. Otherwise the girl is a wallflower.

Two such young girls were the epitome of that. They sat for hours on low stools consulting a huge German fashion catalogue, ticking off the clothes and the shoes that they were going to order by mail. These model garments were for a social life that did not exist, or at least was in its infancy. A girl cannot go alone to a party; she must go with a brother or her cousin and when she gets there her brother or her cousin is not so keen to dance with her. So she sits. She accepts. Or she meets a married man. But that is taboo. Somebody told me a story which I then wrote into a little tale:

One day a beautiful girl stood under the palm trees staring out to sea. The man who was very much older came up and whispered how for years he had borne a love for her, and now as he was going away he must confess it to her. Tremble, tremble. She too loved him. A week or two of clandestine meetings. Of course he was married. Of course he loved her. Of course he would write. A last night of infinite excruciating sweetness. Forget-me-not. Never. Ever. The words, the date palm, the sea, to make it all the more lapidary. He goes away. She waits. It is a dark tormenting secret. No one must know. One day she breaks down and tells her best friend. Her best friend does not rebuke her. 'Imagine it, me with a married man and my friend does not tell me how bad I am.'

The days pass, the nights lacerate her.

One day her friend rings up and asks her to come over as she has news. Her friend was standing in her garden under her palm tree staring out to sea when a man, a much older man, a married man stands behind her and says now that he is going away he has to confess this long withheld love. A week or two of delicious clandestine meetings, car drives, canoodling, promises, a last evening of infinite excruciating sweetness. Now the two girls are holding on to a rather short-lived dream when the phone rings and a third girl asks the second girl to come over as she has something terrible to tell her. The song they listen to says:

> I waited
> and I will wait
> hoping that in my wait
> there is obedience.
> I have been suppressing my feeling
> in the hope
> that you will have mercy on me.
>
> I am waiting for you
> as a thirsty camel
> searching for water
> in the depth of the desert.

Some of these young girls are bewitching, eyes black as sloes and the thickest luxuriant black hair. Hair so shiny that it seems wet.

The middle-class housewives have their own utopias. Black little shoes, black little shawls, couture from Paris. Bridge and coffee mornings. One says that theirs too is a little Peyton Place. Her elderly cook had slain his niece for infidelity. The modern and the feudal. The Arab women she said were bawdy and outspoken. Only that very day a local woman had called out to her in the market: 'When did you throw that child out of your belly?' The puritanism was another mask.

'Your honour is your rumour,' says the Arab proverb, and this I found to be resoundingly true, particularly of the woman. An Arab woman is a precious thing to her father, her brothers and eventually her husband. She is at one and the same time her husband's preserve, possession and pleasure. She does not go out. She does not go to market, she does not walk in her own garden lest she be espied by another man. She does not see the tailor who makes her capacious dresses – he copies them from a previous dress. For her privacy is a must and almost as important as the men who decree it. One morning, as I walked by the public baths at Buraimi in search of fresh air and the mere sight of a trickle of water, I saw a few women by the side of the bath, washing clothes. Their faces were masked and they were veiled. The photographer who was with me stopped to take a photo, and they scattered, screaming, into the trees. Our guide, who was an immigrant girl, ran too, because she said within seconds they would be back with their fathers or their husbands who would waylay us.

All through my stay I found resistance. The women would not speak to me although I made it clear that I really did not want to cross their bedroom doors. Perhaps

they thought that there was something I longed to know which was outside their experience. At any rate my stay was without that fine correspondence between their life and mine, between our two cultures.

I went one morning to a girls' school and the headmistress asked if she could please know my thoughts, please know what I was going to say. In the same school an American teacher praised the Arab woman's way of life so fulsomely that I found myself party to platitudes that would embarrass the brashest of advertising men. This I found sad, this I find sad.

Going to the hairdresser was a somewhat haphazard experience. A boy of about nine is tidying the place somewhat randomly. The towels have piled up. Years of towels it would seem. Tom Jones is on the cassette singing 'Thank You For the Feeling'. No one really wants to work and I get the feeling I may be there all night. A young girl going by offers me a bite from a bar of chocolate. The stylist is standing directly in front of one of these harsh colour photographs of himself and the resemblance is not striking. He abandons one to light a cigarette and then he is called to the telephone and during that long preamble six or seven more clients have arrived and he breaks off to shake hands with them. Protocol and ennui go side by side. A recalcitrant small child starts to toss magazines up like pancakes. The patron slaps the child. The mother is lost in umbrage and all work – such as it was – is temporarily suspended as everyone watches the battle between child and patron. The child throws a cushion in the air and unfortunately for all of us the flock and the feathers fly about. I will never get out of here. I am going to an ambassadorial dinner. There perhaps informality will prevail and people will talk to me. A self-regarding if somewhat hefty beauty strolls about with her newly blow-dried jet-black hair. She is wearing a black georgette

dress with gold epaulettes. It just misses being chic. Sensing perhaps a certain impatience in me the owner tells me that he has styled all the best people in the world, all the celebrities. Women come in and out from under the drier pointedly ignoring the fact that several other women are waiting in their wet rollers to get in there. As for the one wash basin there is a bevy of people around it. Then something catches my eye and it is the little Egyptian boy who is supposed to be cleaning. He is leaning pensively on the pinnacle of dirty towels and he has assumed a pose that is the very same as if Cartier-Bresson has created him. The proverb says that the understanding of an Arab is in his eyes. It was as if he knew more than he could ever express.

Often the faces and the voices did not match. I wanted to peel their language away – that ready-made language for interviews, speeches, inaugurations and openings and conventions. A language founded on excess. A sheikha being interviewed by a school magazine gave expression to the nobility of Sheikha Fatima. A women's organization is called the Abu Dhabi Society for the Awakening of Woman. I went there one morning and found twenty or thirty taciturn women sitting still. Perhaps they were unnerved by my presence. What can one say about having penetrated a sanctum of sewing machines, knitting wool and homemade nightgowns except that it is very laudable? In the book-case were some English books including eight or nine volumes by Joseph Conrad. He had come a long way from darkest Africa to bright Arabia. One woman wept because her husband was going to hospital that day. A young girl strutted about, her body insinuating itself through the folds of her satin abba. I could see that they were creatures of passion but knew alas that I would not be the recipient of it. In fact I was prepared to believe that their children had all been conceived by a massive immaculate conception. I wonder if they watched me with the same confoundedness as I was watching them. Outside was

a stage of new plywood and a little theatre for visiting foreign artists. I had a longing to see Bette Middler with her afro hair belting out 'Mansions in the Sky'. Later I was told that their favourite film was one showing the private life of the British Royal Family.

In the same school magazine there was an interview with the headmistress and the same mélange of enthusiastic, portmanteau language. The same lack of self-criticism. The same apostolic veneration for their country. I met the good lady one morning much to her surprise. I had an appointment as I thought, but one cannot be sure of anything. In contrast to the other women who wore abbas she wore a balaclava which made me think of Florence Nightingale. She greeted me with apprehension. Why had I come? What shaming things was I going to write? It was then indeed that I envied Mr Thesiger writing about the desert lark and having a guide who sat down with him and told him each little bit of vegetation in the desert – the tribulus, the heliotrope, the tasselled sedge, the salt bush and the abal whose little yellow balls were good for a thirsty camel. Eventually I visited the classroom and when I emerged she was there to ask me to please tell her my thoughts. My few crumbs of thought were that I had seen some disarming young girls and that their English teacher reminded me of those dauntless women who set out for the unknown with plum pudding and woollen vests. The young girls had watched me with a kind of wonder and when I read for them the first pages of my first novel I think they thought that I was an adventuress. Full of silent curiosity. Their eyes shone. A few were already married and two or three were dreaming of professional careers. I told the headmistress that really I had had no thoughts as my brain was suffering setbacks and as soon as I gave voice to a few token words of Arabic her anxiety grew less. I sat and had the ritual coffee in the ritual little dolls' cups. By now I could tell a Persian coffee pot from an Omani from an Iraqi, and there were a few in beaten gold that I faintly coveted.

To the same school had come the dazzling Foreign Minister, His Excellency Mr Ahmad Suweidi, and here too was an account of this written in the same vaporous way. Oh why, I thought, will they not be simpler, why will they not take off their mental veils and speak their thoughts freely? When I met him I felt curiously that the meeting was not actually taking place although for certain it was and I remember the large office, his fine-honed face, the fluent interpreter whom he insisted be present and the various other assistants who came, listened and drifted off again. I clearly remember the speed, brilliance and copiousness of Mr Suweidi's thoughts. He delivered me a kind of speech and yet at the very end, as his many assistants stood in the stance of both politeness and frenzy – he was required in so many other places – he rose like a knight and for some reason perhaps unknown to, perhaps even unobserved by himself, he lifted his long mantle and swished it to one side so that one saw a gaunt skin and a dusk, handsome, sandalled foot. Towards the end of that interview I had said that I felt that the people I spoke to including His Excellency had put feeling aside, had if you like dispensed with it. The charming interpreter smiled but intervened. I was being unfair. Perhaps it is a difference in cultural viewpoint but I cannot believe that a handsome cosmopolitan man with vast power, vast wealth, a new wife, new children, a former private life, is not prey to feeling. Shared aspirations, developing nations and national income are themes that even the most elect cannot keep thinking about all the time.

Each day I would ask the driver about the return of the Ruler. He seemed so intrinsic to his country that not to have met him would be like having a legend without a

hero. The driver would then pronounce on the Sheikh's merits.

'Sheikh Zayed does not put the money into his own bank but into the country and the many projects.'

'If the Sheikh is glad you will notice he is glad.'

'If the Sheikh is sad you will notice he is sad.'

'The Sheikh cannot put a lie into his own heart.'

'The Sheikh make Abu Dhabi a green garden.'

Each morning as we drove more or less purposelessly through this medley of roundabouts and streets he would regale me with the Sheikh's qualities, plus information about power stations, high-voltage electricity, the satellite station, blood donation and mother and child care. Each morning I would express tepid amazement and learn yet again the import of one of these concrete palaces and look again at the little saplings that were being fed with the precious, expensive desalinated water from the drip-feed hoses.

I was brought to the Petroleum Exhibition. A morning's treatise on crude oil, lightest and best-quality oil, offshore and onshore concessions and natural gas. I little thought that the study of rock and soil samples, the formation of a drill, swamps or the simulated sounds of the echoes of sands would engross me, but they did. Here after all was my reality. The price of life or the commodity I might or might not afford was being partially decided, right here. I felt, without being able to experience it, the indemnity of money, the power it must impart, the possible arrogance and the dread that it might run out. Money after all is like love or misfortune – cyclical, constant only in its inconstancy.

The information about the oil and how they treat it issued from cassettes, and the data was interspersed with choir music, seismic music, trumpet music and the sounds of running water or perhaps running oil. As I learn of the link between inland oil fields and coastal shipping, I feel useless, replete. Writing is for another realm. Oil is the touchstone of the society, the voice says, and goes on to say that oil has changed the world picture. The ancient East once ruled over the West and now for an ecological reason she does it again. It only needs a dip into history to teach us the see-saw of power. I already knew that at night I would dream of pumps, dumpers and stone crushers, and I did.

As I wandered through the dark spacious air-conditioned room, hearing the full, implosive, glorious saga, I had a feeling that I was being drawn into a cavern. Would this go on for ever? Might I have to come here each morning losing hope as I did of meeting men and women? I learn that oil was probably first formed as marine organisms hit the sea bed, and that oil was discovered through the careful and exigent study of rock and soil samples and that its presence down there sent echoes from the deep, back to the earth. I thought of babies in the womb, mites, that sent echoes to their mothers and sometimes those close to their mothers. Was I not going a little mad?

'Please, if you would, please,' the guide would say as I moved on to the next batch of bright progressive photographs, some of workmen in workmen's perfectly tattered clothing, of conversion plants, degassing plants, reservoirs, ships, cars, smiling multiracial faces and attendants such as I rarely see at petrol pumps.

Back in the hotel I met a young Englishman who looked the epitome of poet and traveller. He had a hawk and most nights slept out of doors in the desert. He told me

the things that a Bedouin considers noble, that have no price but may be obtained as a present:

Falcon
Saluki
Horse
Camel

At last a journey. The following morning we set out for Al 'Ain, Sheikh Zayed's birthplace and spiritual home, a fertile place because of the water that flows underground from mountains. I consult the guidebook and learn that the grey steel bridge we are crossing costs $3 million and measures 1,400 by 85 feet. Soon we are on the expensive jammed four-lane highway – the national artery, as it is called. Tracks of greenery in the middle. The traffic is tremendous, cars, lorries, articulated lorries. The driver is piqued because we are asked to stop at a police check-point. It does not fit in with his self-image of being the greatest advocate of his country. Very soon the desert. Not of course uninterrupted desert because in between there is a building site or a radio mast or advertisements for tyres, office equipment and a cigarette that promises a magic intake of gold. The driver would point to where there was going to be a gymnasium or a settlement for Bedouins or where there had been a falcon conference. A huge figure in gypsum adorned the site and I thought of those Irish saints that blessed the passing of the wayward motorist. The traffic was tremendous. On all sides the lorries and the articulated lorries bringing concrete or paving slabs or baths or mobile homes or water. Little tufts of grass on the surface of the desert, as thin as a needle.

My first experience of the desert was profound, even daunting. What struck me was the scale of it – a visual eternity. A herd of camels, statuesque in their course, were ambling towards a well or away from a well. There were

huts where the men lived who attended to the trees. Sometimes the Bedouin settlements – dun square concrete, like beehives or biscuit tins.

The desert drives other thoughts away. It is compelling. Here it was orange with the sun beating down upon it. There it was brown near the waterpipes, and in the distance a pale, bleached, relentless arena that went on for ever. Breathtaking, as well as frightening. It is the immensity of the desert that daunts one. Did God make this world? So little to see, so little to distract, nothing to cling to, a sort of silence of the ethos. Mr Robin Bidwell was right. A person could not pretend here. So little, so much. A figure, perhaps a man, yes probably a man, with a cloth on his head bound tight and over it a bunch of faggots. Where did he get them and where is he going? To comprehend eternity perhaps one should live like this. I ached for my own house, for my fireside, for a rug over my shoulders. I felt transplanted. Now the colour had changed and some sand was red and some was ochre. Then suddenly, a factory, for making silicate bricks. Near Al 'Ain a university being built that is a model of Cairo University. Egypt perhaps is most responsible for the architecture here, but not the Egypt of the pharaohs, of tiered structures and red sandstone, not the Egypt of the gilded dome but the Egypt like today's world – modern, costly, supposedly functional, and without one spark of divine inspiration.

It was Friday, sabbath day. In the hotel in Al 'Ain, the unattached ever-hopeful bachelors and the families were out in full flood. Children raced through the dining room, saris shone under the electric light that hung from gilt boxes, waiters jostled with each other as they carried water jugs while the rapacious guests helped themselves to delights from the vast buffet. All the food looked like confectionery, childhood food. Everything being a little too ornate. Turkey had a curious iced glaze over it and bits of angelica to add extra decoration. The pâté was squeezed into cases that made it seem one was going to partake of chocolate ice-cream. The meat dishes had segments of orange on the top and the confectionery itself was like eiderdowns, all white and vapid. People ate huge quantities, going back for more and more.

I was glad to be there, but for another reason. I had gone to Al 'Ain particularly to meet Colonel Sir Hugh Boustead, a soldier, a traveller and one of Sheikh Zayed's earliest advisers, and I knew that by nightfall I would be on his ranch looking at the Sheikh's horses and talking to a man whose sensibilities I hoped I understood. Unlike me he had been present at the conception and the birth of the new Abu Dhabi and he had a sympathy for it that I had not found, although in all truth I groped for it.

My appointment was 'being arranged'. By now I knew that appointments took their own mysterious course and that it would be the height of folly and impertinence to rush them or to ask for a precise time. I left the dining room and sat in the air-conditioned lobby, and relatively content, I would read snatches of Colonel Sir Hugh Boustead's book *Wind in the Morning*; then to rest my eyes I would look out of the window at the ranges of mountain that he described as violet. Over there was Oman where I also hoped to go. Such a glut of hopes. These were real mountains and not just conglomerations of sand. Substantial mountains towering up. At that moment pale lilac, or so my notebook says. I realized that I liked mountains and that perhaps they fitted in with some childhood fable of the other world, the world beyond. I also realized that I wanted to go to Oman. I had seen beautiful old stone fortresses and I had seen photographs of faces more honed, more finished and more heroic than any others. But it would come, just as Sir Hugh Boustead would come. I recalled the story on which Camus based his essay, *The Myth of Sisyphus*, the man whose wearisome destiny it was to heft a rock up a mountain only to find

when he reached the summit that it rolled back down of its own accord, and that he had to follow down and faithfully repeat his action that would then be abnegated by the retoppling of the rock. Camus had made the profoundly sane remark that one must imagine Sisyphus happy on his journey back down the mountain. Of course I was happy, expecting as I did the gallant figure of Sir Hugh to come through the open door. On the back of his book there was the photo of him on horseback the very picture of bravery, and as I waited I thought with such excitement of driving out into the empty country, not just as a sightseer but as a guest. Oh yes, I added nightfall and the stars, the horses, the stables, a fire, a drink, adding English creature comforts to desert mystery. A few holidaymakers sat by the pool, four fanatics played tennis, three of them wearing handker-chiefs as headgear. There was piped music. The heat was glaring. The boy in the hairdresser's had a bridal party and God help anyone else who needed a hairdo that day. Women with thick black compilations of hair sat in wait. The bachelors on their way in or out of the bar bestowed me with not unsuggestive looks. I was thirsty. I felt like a celebration even though there was no visible cause for one and no reason. I thought of Chekhov dying at Baden-Baden and rather rashly ordered a half-bottle of cham-pagne. It was an absurdity. For one thing an ice bucket was wheeled towards me and for another I now received all the attention that I had been so assiduously avoiding. I asked them to bring two glasses and prayed that Sir Hugh Boustead would come striding up the steps or if necessary come up on one of his horses. Anything to take the embarrassment out of this ludicrous act. It was as if hotel life ceased as observers stopped to witness the opening of a half-bottle of champagne in a vast lobby on a sweltering afternoon. I do not think the waiter had vast experience of champagne. In all innocence he complained to me that the cork was too stiff. He fetched a corkscrew. By now I was on my feet ready to run from the explosion. With my thumb I began to indicate how it could be done. A gentleman from the Yemen who worked on a construction site suggested getting a hammer. Everyone watched. Almost everyone laughed. A few other waiters strolled by, pretending not to observe the débâcle that was going on. I would ask the waiter to leave it for a moment as if by some kind of miracle the situation would right itself. All I wanted now was to have it removed with as little to-do as possible. The sun which had no penumbra flashed shamelessly on the gold-painted walls, over which peacocks had been painted in blue with gold, with multicoloured tails. Any minute he must come. Except that he didn't. The champagne was warm and without sparkle.

At six o'clock I decided to set out for his home and proceeded to inquire about a taxi. Here again the full reality of my situation struck home to me. I was a woman, alone. The assistant manager said the journey would not be safe. He bent his head and muttered something about isolated roads. I said was it not safe? It was not that I wanted a fulsome story about either rape or gang rape, I merely wanted to know precisely what was unsafe about it. Would I be robbed or worse? He would not divulge. He looked at me covertly and in my mind which by then was a little askew I could imagine that he was considering my rape potential, which of course he was not. He said that I must wait till the next day. I couldn't. I had schedules. That uncustomary word sprang to my lips and brought in him a reaction that he understood. The modern world, business, schedules. He rose to it. He said I must wait till next day. He said that he would come with me and the merry thought did occur that since I was not to trust these men, why trust him? He changed his jacket and just as we were going down the steps one of the young loping boys from the hotel followed to ask my name. Then he handed me a telegram. It had been lying there all day, waiting in its cubbyhole, just as I was waiting in mine. Like many another thing this had echoes of Franz Kafka. It was succinct, it could or then again it could not be addressed to me in particular. It simply said: 'SIR HUGH BOUSTEAD IS ILL AND WILL SEE NO ONE TODAY.' Who had sent it? Why had they not told me? When did it arrive? Will he be ill tomorrow? Irish rage reached my extremities, causing the manager to walk away and causing me to follow after him to ask purposelessly why I hadn't got the message earlier.

His office is crammed with cardboard boxes and he has the effrontery to apologize for this, then he picks up a comic and starts to read it. He said there is to be a barbecue supper that night and a beautiful movie featuring Raquel Welch. I ask if he has already seen the movie, to which he says no, which in turn makes me wonder how he can be so sure it's beautiful. We are getting nowhere. I storm out of the lobby and in a mixture compounded of frustration, pique and near despair decide to take the advice of a serene Arab gentleman in robes whose beauty is quite remarkable. If T. E. Lawrence is willing to be smitten by a Bedouin beauty then so am I. He tells me that he is private secretary to a sheikh and should I wish it he will take me there for conference at once. The assistant manager who has come into the lobby again shakes his head discomfitingly. The Egyptian girl presides like a model behind the desk and looks on at the proceedings with a vexing languor. I blame her most of all for keeping my telegram from me. In fact my experience with Egyptian girls throughout was anything but happy. They all seemed to keep me from me and my destiny. Sheikh Zayed's wife Sheikha Fatima was screened by Egyptian girls, and when I am able to afford a bodyguard in my own life I will think very seriously of getting a bevy of them. So here I am at sundown being invited by a strange man to meet a sheikh whom I do not know. Very felicitous. I have been

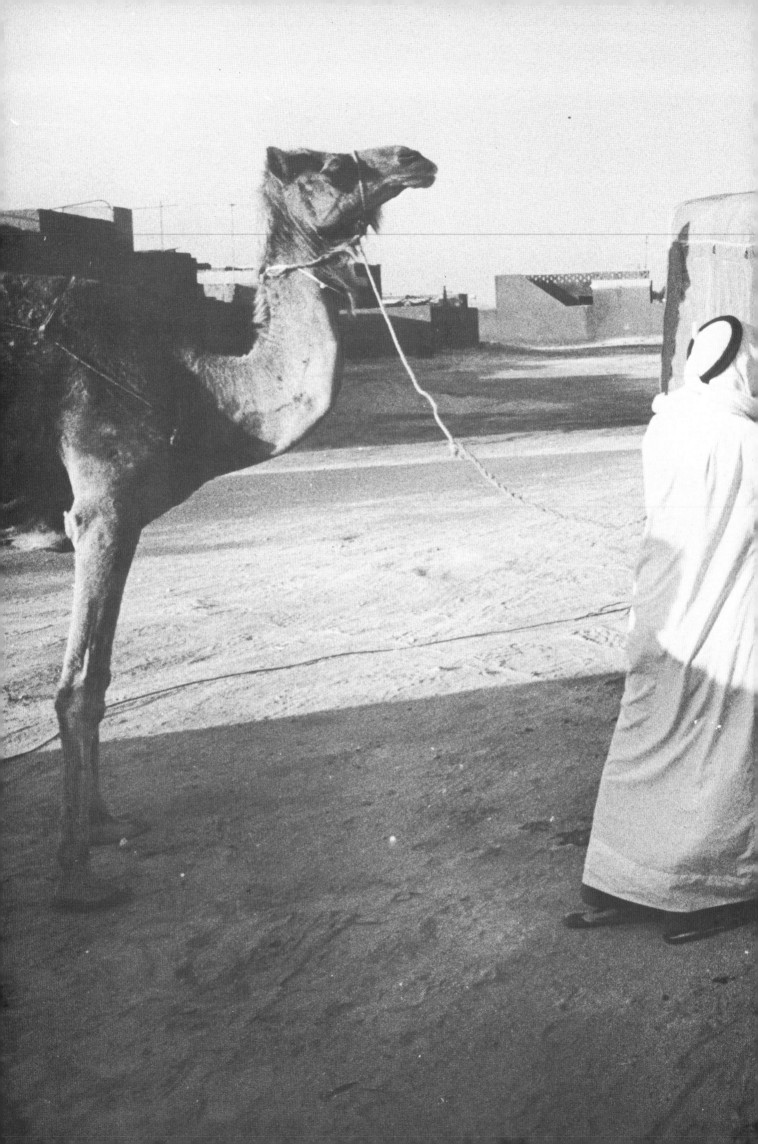

trying for days to meet other people and failing with a fertility that is inducing paranoia. So I am at last progressing. The manager says I go at my own risk.

We set off in a Land-Rover. Two coffee cups rest above the dashboard and as we drive they clang together but do not break. The sheikh's secretary speaks perfect English. I am almost tempted to ask him what he intends to do with me. I don't. We drive through a city that is suburbia stuck in the desert: lock-up shops whose wares are impossible to describe, with dwellings above. Of all things I see a sign for Kentucky Chicken. It was such inauspicious unlyrical things that made me long for Piccadilly Circus though normally I eschew it. There was a beautiful mosque and an unbeautiful cement construction containing a stopped clock. Downtown Al 'Ain was no Zanzibar. Just to add to the mystery he suddenly stopped outside one of those settlements for Bedouins, alighted, edged his way past some chickens and goats and called to some children within. I still don't know why.

As we approach the sheikh's house I am positively disappointed because it too has the prevailing dilapidated look. Leonardo da Vinci and his entire school would have plenty of scope here. There is a high concrete wall with a honeycomb décor on top, there are old barrels, clutter and bits of machinery, or the relics of machinery. Yet as I pass through the gateway grandeur looms. I think it is the opposite to Ireland where prosperous-looking exteriors often belie bare boards or at best a pebbledash bungalow. I am brought to the quarters that the sheikh has built for receiving. It is fronted with patterned marble and the door is wide open. The carpet that hits the eye is brightness itself and the edge of the carpet juts like fringing beyond the doorstop. Inside are the huge pneumatic new sofas that make one feel an audience is nigh. At the far end of the room there is a sideboard along which are placed photos of three sheikhs in glaring colour. At once the servant arrives with a huge platter of fruit and my escort presses me to take a banana. Presently his master arrives. He is in white and barefoot. He sits cross-legged on an armchair and is told what I am doing. His eyes are dark and canny. The houseboy arrives with a coffee pot. Then almost at once with Lipton's teabags in long glasses. It is already sweetened. Tea followed by coffee is not my idea of a treat and now that it's dark I am dreaming of whisky or brandy or even palm toddy. The sheikh expresses interest in my arrival and says he would like to discuss all things with me. Victory. At last a real conversation is going to ensue. The occidental and the oriental mind will find a place and a point at which they can converse. I say that I am interested to know how his present and his past life conflict and complement each other. I realize that it is only a matter of years since he lived in the desert. Also the bareness and rawness of the reception room tell me that he is not at ease in such a place and that he never will be. I ask the question. His secretary interprets it. He looks at me. They have a way of looking at you after a question that makes you feel you have perhaps overreached. He smiles at me, he speaks to the interpreter. I receive my answer. My answer is that by asking such a question he has to tell me that in his opinion I have come in search of spilt milk. I think of Premier Khrushchev and his bulwark of proverbs and I know that it augurs badly. What ensues is a compendium of wise-saws and clichés such as that old customs are disappearing, that in the past Bedouins managed their difficulties between themselves since they had no police, that a Bedouin war could be about such diverse things as stealing a date or defecting to another tribe, that Bedouins honoured their treaties and so forth. He watches as I write down these things. He sees perhaps a sinking in me. Suddenly he

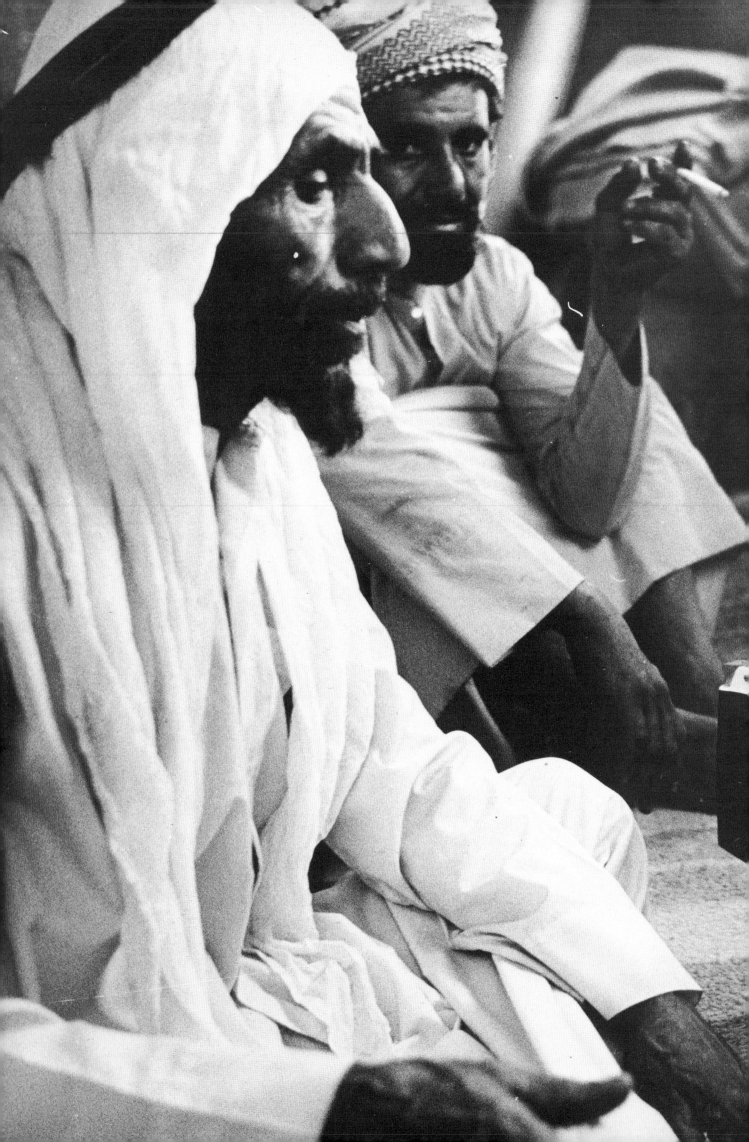

jumps up and goes out to prayer and I ask the interpreter what the prayers are, and, deliberating, he explains about God the Compassionate, the Almighty and All-Merciful. One's own faith begins to be a little less absolute when one is confronted by other people equally certain that theirs is right. The sheikh comes back in, and slowly, we can become a little more personal in our discussion and he nods sagely and then renods. So I take the plunge and ask what it feels like to live in a spacious house bounded by four walls when once he lived in a tent. He says the current of civilization is changing.

He will not answer any question that pertains to wives, morality, religion, family or even that elusive thing, happiness. He says he may go wrong by endeavouring to answer. Then he picks up *Arabian Sands* which I had brought with me and he says that some of the points in that book are true. Suddenly it is as if he had decided to speak to me. A whole portmanteau of words is being told to the interpreter who is now smiling and I am beginning to smile. Not for long. The revelation was thus. He dissertated on the fact that one man may be happy doing a crime, another may be happy eating, another may be happy doing good and that therefore happiness is a multifarious thing. I agree and somewhat breathlessly have it interpreted that I would really like to know a little something about himself. His eyes narrow, he almost laughs and then he folds his hands together slowly while he prepares to embark on yet another impersonal dissertation.

After we have left I learn from his secretary that he is not married, that he lives on camel's milk, that he owns several buildings in the town which he lets to traders and that his 'hobby' is supporting one hundred poor families over the mountains in Oman.

I then ask the secretary if *he* could tell me a little about life, and without seeming too scatalogical I tell him that for instance we are interested in the psychological situation of having many wives. I have made a solemn vow to skirt the mention of anything sexual. He says he is opposed to many wives because more than one wife can be a headache. I say how. Again I expect something that will startle me. He says if you give one wife a red skirt you must give the other wife a red skirt and not a green or a blue or any other colour. Then he describes a man he knows with four wives who diligently sleeps with one each night, always in turn, but he says it is not really a peaceful house because the latest and the youngest wife wants to be favourite. He himself has one wife, but who knows that one day he may take another!

He is happier once the conversation gets on to his days in the desert. For this he is genuinely nostalgic, even bereaved. He says how simple life was, compared with the city bustle. We are, I ought to say it, in a small town with various huxter shops, two cinemas, a mosque, a four-faced defunct clock and a little trail of fairy lighting that has survived from some wedding or carnival. He said how he liked to live wild, not having to change clothes all the time, not having to wash all the time, walking miles for water, then miles back, drinking camel's milk, occasionally eating goat or gazelle, and having for amusement the one fantastic night of dancing and chanting when there would be a wedding among the tribe. Like all Arabs he delighted in recounting the fact of the abounding generosity of the desert Bedouin. He pointed out to me that were I to be their visitor they would slaughter for me their most valuable goat, that is to say a young goat which was also a she-goat, and that they would slaughter as many she-goats as there were strange guests. I said that at least in one field the female was the most prized and he laughed, and for some reason said that women did not like the desert, that women did not have the innate solitude that could endure the desert, except perhaps for old women who liked to sleep under the moon.

I did not like the prospect of going back alone to the hotel. Though from the brochure it was anyone's dream – a place that glittered after dark like diamond on black velvet. I believed I was returning to a room that was modern, air conditioned, with spectacular view of oasis, desert sand and ancient mountains. The specialities that were being prepared for dinner for my discriminating self had all the exotica of the *Arabian Nights*.

Up in my room I witnessed an odd thing. I had come up from the bar because Arab men like Irishmen are not always the best when they drink heavily. They tend to shout - their old disturbed psyches come marching in.

Depriving myself of Raquel Welch and the roast suckling kid I thought to have an omelette and stand on my balcony to observe these oases and mountains that were my 'open sesame'. And what did I hear? Down below the noise of the drinkers, the strains of music starting up in the discothèque and on the far side of the wall of my bedroom a zealous Muslim chanting the Koran in a low, unending monotone. He chanted for hours, and in the end I knelt down myself and began to intone a few wan prayers. We differ because of clothes, climate, food and above all language, but we forget that God got in there first! Religious difference is perhaps the most unyielding of all. Islam means to surrender. Yet Islamic religion seems righteous, robust, fulsome and sure of itself. As mindful of secular matters as of supernatural ones. Richard Burton thought it to be the only real religion in the world, yet he did not convert to it. Napoleon also flirted with the idea of converting but was dissuaded for two very good reasons – abstinence from drink, and circumcision. Its one test is conduct. Its followers are dissuaded from usury, strong drink and gambling. Power is its handmaiden. The thunderous power of righteousness. Muhammad was a military man. His faith-

ful were inured to battle. His creed did not say turn the other cheek.

I certainly saw more manifestation of religion there than in the West. I have no idea how deeply it has pervaded their lives but I do know at sundown on the roads cars would suddenly stop and men jump out for the praying ritual. In fact the men seemed to observe it more assiduously than the women and I thought of Ireland where the reverse is true and, at Christmas, when the women do a crib crawl the men do a pub crawl! As I lay in my hotel bedroom I was struck by the hypnotic quality of the incantation, by its power of self-hypnosis.

The next morning in Al 'Ain I walked around the museum tracing a life or a mode of life that they too know is passing. Here behind glass were the veils, the mask made of Indian paper, the long shielding bloomers, the longer dress, the swathing abba designed for protection against heat and cold and against concupiscent eyes. Here too the seashells used for feeders, the circumcision stool, the model palm tree and a summary of its many uses. On the wide shoulder-blade of a camel some words were scratched, words that were like notes of music, and the ink used was from the summer tree. The horse saddles were covered in sumptuous velvet decked with bobbins with tassels and bells of gold. The camel saddle was of woven cloth with tassels but no gold. Then the jewellery – the dark burnished necklaces that would extend almost to the navel, the golden nose-rings, the bride's chest, the pots of henna, the various herbs to open the pores, to whiten the body and to make it clean. Weapons, swords with jewelled handles, daggers, silver sheaths, instruments for blood letting and the helmets of thick chain-mail. A world both simplified and complex, a world at once cruel and ornate, and a world that will pass. I came out into the blistering

heat and felt refreshed at the promise of being brought to the baths and oasis of Buraimi.

My meaning of the word oasis will never be quite the same again. Here in noonday heat I walked down a dry mud slope where there were trees and little cement baths of water in which people languored. These baths were toy-like in their scale. The men were doing their toiletries while in others there were little naked girls dark as Africa, washing each other's hair, splashing or paddling. The trees overhead barely stirred. A cock crowed. This little oasis did not reflect the modernity of the hotel or the busy helter-skelter of Abu Dhabi. It was people washing, thinking, reflecting, above all people committed to privacy. Further on where the women washed their clothes there was not a sound, just the mere sigh of a tree in the daytime scarcely stirring.

At the hotel a young boy waited for me in secret. We had met the night before, had had a few whiskies and talked about romances. He had a letter to show me, a love letter from a local woman. He laughed nervously as he read bits of it and then had to tuck it away as someone eavesdropped. It was like being told a serial but one had to wait for every tantalizing line.

Tell me words
as if it is wrong
as if you are lying
from you it will be very sweet.
I will be killed by your shape
I am still in the love a child
between me and you
there are seas and mountains
and still you did not understand me
I don't like to be a clown
and if I remember a day
that I say to you I love you
forget it
Because it means I love you more
Apologize my looking to you
as if it is wild
But in it there is light.
I look to you
to let my eyes glutton on you
and also to eat from your beauty.
To take your picture into my womb
The less of you seeing
makes me clasp you more
And if you don't want me to I will stop
but today I think I love you forever.

Then I sat on the steps to wait for my driver. The air had been unbearably tense as if something was due to burst. Without warning the rain came. A savage downfall. Vertical sheets of it, so that sky and mountain were now like legendary giants lost in the throes of mist. The lightning that started up was forked, frequent and so carnival-like I would have believed that pieces of the gold-filigreed jewellery were stuck into the heavens. The peals of thunder sent terror into one, and within no time the surface of the road was like a lake through which the cars and the truck splurged. The trees came into their own and quickly acquired a proud bright sheen, the sort of sheen they have in a valley in Ireland. No longer were they like dusty quills, and now in the rain and with the weight of rain the fronds swayed. On the surface of the lodged water the bubbles were like moonstones, big and glistening. You could see the red flowers open and swell before your very eyes. One felt - at least I felt - grateful that flowers, grass and sand were getting this rare baptism. The flies came out. Was this the deluge? It did seem as if it might go on for ever.

But it was short-lived. And while it was still raining the sun began to press through, the mountains were restored to their former shapes and the whole thing was as if a rain meteor had passed through and quickly vanished. But spirits were a little better. The tautness that the desert induced in a stranger had been mollified, and as I say, the paths and the bushes and the trees had got a soaking while elsewhere the herbs and the thorn bush would grow a little stronger and make better pasture for the camels.

I was glad to be going back to Abu Dhabi. I had a vision that there would be envelopes in my room letting me know about appointments, about the helicopter, about Sheikh Zayed, about many things. Of course I over-imagined. But there was something. I had made a friend, an engineer whom I had met one morning on a site. He

had left a bag of almonds. They were fresh, clean-tasting and they spoke to me of one of my most desired landscapes – forest.

My first venture to a sheikha's house was just the same as if I'd been brought simultaneously to a convent, Woolworth's and a storybook cut-out of Eastern romance. The furnishings were gaudy. The fabric smelt new. It was like one of those foyers that led to one of those grand cinemas in the 1940s or 1950s. Bright red and bright yellow. Thick woven carpet with rugs laid over them, the chandeliers full on. Here no man ventures except the husband of the sheikha and here the women perfume themselves with sandalwood. A lot of women all peering at me behind their masks. At times I felt at a disadvantage. The chief sheikha was a young girl of nineteen who had been married at fourteen. To my first and obvious question about resistance, even dismay, at having a husband chosen for her she said – as so many others said – 'We accept.'

One of her English teachers explained it differently. They see no one else, meet no other man, except members of the family, and so have not been given the pick and choose that we are used to. It is impossible for us in the West with our freedom of movement, adventure and choice to conceive of a happy woman whose social life is ordained by men. But on they go. Naturally the women form staunch friendships and for all I know love friendships too. The urge for love is so strong that we humans will stop at no object on which to fasten it. Nor would such love carry the same odium as adultery. Not that there could be adultery unless the woman were to sleepwalk. They meet all the time, they talk all the time, they drink sweet tea or coffee and they move in their artificially lit palaces with a sort of slow grace. No haste here, no reminder of the modern world except for the telephones which are as favourite with them as toys.

Eyes peered out at me from between the slits of their dun-gold cardboard masks. Hair was black, thick, often frizzy and disguised under a veil. Feet were bare. Toenails were painted and toes as well as ankles were decorated with henna in patterns of twigs or little trees. Lots of jewellery. Bracelets, necklaces and ankle bracelets. There were about a dozen of us – some laughing, some watching me warily, some serving. It is easy to grow fat, what with the sweetmeats, the leisure and the lack of exercise. Indian yoga, or for that matter Indian spirituality, has not permeated their way of life. We take the orange juice from gold goblets and slowly we sip it. Next thing in the ritual is the burnt sandalwood on its bed of charcoal carefully passed around. This constituted the only flippant moment. After I had breathed it and expressed my delight in it I was then told I could stand up and one of them held it under my skirts so that the fumes of perfume could float up. This called for laughter. So too did my question about jealousy. If a man has another wife – his religion allows him four – how does a loving wife bear it? At first they demurred. Then one who was old said she had forgotten all about her jealousy, but one who was young said sometimes she felt so wildly jealous she believed she would go mad. One said that she conquered it by asking for more precious gifts. The presents their husbands bring them back from their travels are of great importance, a test and guarantee of love. They would get up, move away as if to some rendezvous, and return again.

They moved slowly, almost corpulently. I ask one of the young girls to tell me a dream. She said a dream is secret and one must never be told, not even to one's own husband. Sealed lips. Only to herself does she confide. Looking around at them I wondered about their thoughts and I felt, and perhaps this is mere conjecture, that their

thoughts were not as myriad as mine. I would not swap my life for theirs but I could see that they were not restless. They did not have to strive. They were surrounded by each other and showed the fondness and the titteriness that young girls in convents display. Young, that is it. Still young.

For the most part I fared worse with the women than with the men. The women I found reticent in the extreme. Either they refused to see me, or if they saw me as did a young lady official, they went on with their work, their telephone calls as if I were not there. In fact I began to be in some doubt about my own existence. This particular young woman gave me three interviews but always with other people, and always so that she was either making phone calls, receiving phone calls or once making a madeira cake for her family. How I railed about my predicament. I was not, like Mr Doughty, Mr Wilfred Blunt or Mr Thesiger, permitted to travel with men and share the hardship and the adventure, but neither was I like Lady Mary Wortley Montagu who in Constantinople in the early eighteenth century met sultanas in their rooms and in their bath-houses, and so, observant of their privacy, saw their hoarded jewels, that were as big as turkey eggs.

I am a woman
Why am I given breasts
Am I my father's girl

The poem says. But they did not say it. They did not join in it. Of whom are they afraid? I do not think it is simply of their husbands. It is far deeper. It is rooted in their taboo. Mr Burckhardt in his travels between 1812 and 1817 commented on the necessity for a Bedouin girl to foster prudery and reticence. Whatever her sentiments with respect to a lover she could not condescend to let him know them. The

firm assurance of her honour and her chastity must influence his heart, and since his mind was strong and sound, not sickly or depraved like a townsman, it was certain that her good virtues once impressed upon him would take a hold of him. His view of her being paramount.

Even when chosen to be his bride she had at first to resist, to defend herself with stones, to inflict wounds on the young men who were to carry her to her new husband, for according to that custom the more she kicked, the more she cried, the more she resisted, the more was she held in esteem – and even when the abba was thrown over her and she heard the climactic words, 'O none shall cover thee but him,' she was still to resist and be taken by force. She was mounted upon the camel held down, led to his tent and after the marriage brought to a recess in his house. As the marriage was consummated she continued to cry. Some brides had to be held down. Next day if she could she would flee again to the safety of the mountains where he would go in search of her and she would flee again and again. Only when she was well advanced in pregnancy did she consent to live with him. Denial was her greatest boon, self-denial. To jump from that to free choice, sexual initiation, a frank admission of sexuality, is to make an insuperable leap. The fugitive instinct is still in her but added to it are the twentieth-century demands, the outside enjoinders to develop.

The lore and literature pertaining to the Eastern woman has been twofold and wildly contradictory. On the one hand the Koran is laden with moral stricture insisting on piety and reticence, demanding from her silence at the one time in her life when one would think she ought to be let speak – upon being asked to marry. Her silence signified her consent. She is the man's subject, God having gifted him above her. The man is to scold her if she is rebellious, or to leave her alone in her bed and beat

her. 'Your wives are your fields, go in, therefore, to your field as you will.'

On the other hand the Arabian tales translated by Sir Richard Burton abound in the saucy and the lascivious. The woman is constantly depicted as the lewd one taking her pleasure conversely or normally as suits her paramour. Women corrupting one another while waiting for the swain and, it would seem, bent on nothing other than sexual cavort, mirth and merriment. No sooner has a husband gone to the bazaar or the confectioner's or the bath-house than she is opening her door to a lover, springing upon him, kissing his hands and feet leading him to her chamber where she joins him in congress. No

sooner has she commenced this than she is putting him through a trap-door to receive another lover on whom she also intends to bequeath the foulest of favours. She is of course frequently found out, frequently foiled and frequently punished for her ill-doing malice. But there is of course a monstrous inconsistency here. If the woman admits mirth and merriment then obviously the man she is with partakes of the same, but such is the swell of opinion and such the slant of patriarchal thought that only *she* is accused of having done the wrong.

Sir Richard Burton, who collected and translated the tales in the *Arabian Nights*, was to have followed up with *The Scented Garden* which was to be a much more thorough and scatalogical work. Here, he said, was a repertory of Eastern wisdom which was to tell all, including how eunuchs were made, describing female circumcision and the practice of men who copulated with their crocodiles. His wife, herself a woman, burnt it after his death, giving as her legitimate reason the voice of his ghost who called from the grave to have it destroyed lest it corrupt the minds of others who would not read it scientifically. A man of science himself, Burton saw the Arabian tales as belonging to a state of civilization when the sexes are at war with each other, women's major armour being their deceit. Perhaps he did not know that he had also assembled a work whose chief influence would be the arousal and sustainment of male virility.

In today's affluence the men are most certainly the overlords. The woman is now materially cared for and yet confined to her own quarters. When Sheikh Zayed brought his wife to London he had a shop closed so that she could buy things in the utmost privacy. This incident has in it the deadly accuracy of fairy-tale in that it combines wonder with concealment. A statement that struck me far more than all the rhetoric and diffuseness that I was given were the paintings by a young woman of 'The Women of

Abu Dhabi'. Still veiled and still barely perceptible, they stand or crouch in their interiors from which they show no signs of escaping. They are contemplative and their abodes have all the suggestiveness of the cloister. The interiors of their houses are brown, enclosed and sunken. High up as high as the sky was the window. The window was in fact the sky. They would have to fly in order to get out. But the world outside is perhaps one they would recoil from.

We set out for Liwa Desert early one morning. An oasis where the Bani Yas, the tribe of the Ruler, once lived, and eked existence from the dates while in the interior, and from pearl fishing when they joined the fleets in the summer.

Soon the helicopter was scudding over the city and its sprawling outskirts, and in the most sudden and radical way we were presently introduced to the real desert. To say this was startling is not to give an adequate impression of what it did to one – the very mind was turning into sand. I had read of immense plains strewn with numberless undulating hills, and sand with not a trace of vegetation to animate it or a bird to off-set the calm. But to read is one thing, to see is another. Here was the immense sand with each ridge covered over as it were by a wave of shivering sand. The shadow of the helicopter was like a beetle on its surface. Some of the dunes like breasts and some like buttocks. In the underdrop of each dune a flash of red-gold. Little bits of grass or thorn or herbage pitiful in their sparseness. My eyes look up, down, left and right, and on all sides there are these enclosing universes of sand. But over it all an unspeakable wizard strangeness. One's images are to be infused by this.

When we arrive and I step out of the helicopter it was like stepping into a boiler. To walk on sand is quite a shock. To walk on deep sand, that is. It is like wading into sea. How do these men walk for miles and miles to get water? I find myself sinking and knew that at night I would return to that falling sensation. A constant tension between staying upright and sinking into it. All around the yellow colours that for me are the colours of the mind. At one point the sand sedately rising in an incline and seeming like a Titian cloak spread out to welcome us. It is more authoritative and more vast than any artist or any architect could fashion. Never have I felt such brightness, such a naked assault on the cornea and on the senses. I was sure that I was levitating.

Young boys from the army training college rushed forward to welcome us. They swarmed round us, eager to see new faces and to have news. Their life there is circumscribed but they are well paid. It was months since any of them had seen a member of the opposite sex and I wanly remembered how Vera Lynn roused the troops with her songs but all I could do was smile and ask how they liked it. They were lonely. They were bored. They trained, they played football, they ate, they slept. Two of them were learning English from a book. They dreamed of cities the way we dream of paradise. Then a young boy of about ten or eleven arrived in a jeep and he was of a quite different metal. Born and bred there. To him the desert was noble and even the date-palm oasis, where his father was, was secondary. At night, he said, they sat around and talked of camels. I said there is only so much one can say about a camel and he said that was because I hadn't known camels. He shook hands with the men but was reluctant to shake hands with me. He had an innate reserve and a composure that was startling. Could we go to meet his father? He said his father was a two-hour drive away, tending the date palms. After some coaxing we got him into the helicopter and seeing him sit up beside the pilot with earphones on I can only guess the contrast it was for him. Suddenly to be seeing the desert spread out before

him like Mr Eliot's 'patient etherized upon a table'. When he saw the scattering of trees tall and unprepossessing beneath the very blue sky he lost his restraint and clapped with glee.

His father was there waiting. A fine, old man with a carved face, wearing a tweed jacket. His first excited remark was that he would kill a camel for me. He took my hand and we went down a sanded slope to his hut. There is a way of walking on sand and one must not be afraid of it, he said. His sons dragged blankets into the hut and in there a little breeze rustled the fronds of the roof. His wife was bent over a little stove with her mask and veils on, and a positive window display of gold jewellery hanging about her neck. She gave the coffee flask to her son and ritually he poured tiny drops into each cup and ritually we drank. The desert. The real desert with not a sound of anything. The old man had cadaverous cheeks and a sort of haze over his eyes but he emanated welcome. He said I must stay for as long as I liked.

It was amazing how cool the interior was while outside the sun was scalding. I got some intimation of what it was like not to live in a house but to live in a hut, to sit on the floor to feel the passage of air from one opening to the opposite, to lie on the mattress at night. It had a sort of freedom. Yet of course one has to be bred to the desert and I was not. I asked him if he thought I could live in the desert. He was certain that I could. His love of the desert and his recommendation of it as a way of life was absolute in him. The alertness that desert knowledge requires was in him. Bred from a stock that could tell his own camel from far off on the horizon, or by looking at the dead embers of a fire would know how many persons had been there, how many camels, and how many women. An accumulation of knowledge derived as much from absence as from presence. Knowing when to speak, when to be silent. As used to loneliness as a person can be.

No face is forgotten. He invited me back and said that I could send a telex to let them know. It was as if he had been born and bred to the idea of telexes and modern communication. Yet I knew that if I did come back and that if he were there he would know me. The desert mind is not crammed, not cluttered, and not overlaid by each new happening.

By the time we left the sun had gone down and the desert had taken on another aspect altogether. All over was a pale silver light, and one that was not far from ghostly. I think they were sad to see us go, and I was sad to leave them in that fairy light. They would talk about the camels, or so his son had said.

Back in my hotel room I looked at the various books, and the various accounts of camels, their roaring and the ruckling, the long haired, the short haired, the black camel such as the noble and solitary maiden rides.

'Guard well thy camel else the thief will leave thee to perish in the dreary plain' – as vital as that to a man, more vital than human company or food or thought, as vital as he himself. Should a camel run away the owner can trail it by its footsteps for many hours, and can know by its droppings what it has eaten and when. The weaning of a camel is harsh – a piece of wood is driven into the palate and comes out at the nostrils. Or a young camel has sharp wood put across its nostrils so as to prick the mother, who then rejects her young.

I began to feel fonder of these enduring beasts whom no degree of pain induces to refuse a load or to throw it on to the ground. Requiring so little, a few herbs moisten its stomach. In years of scarcity the camels become barren. The strong camel ambling along for five or six days, its hump being its furniture of fat. The Bedouin look for that, that reserve, just as they look at the hind legs to see if there

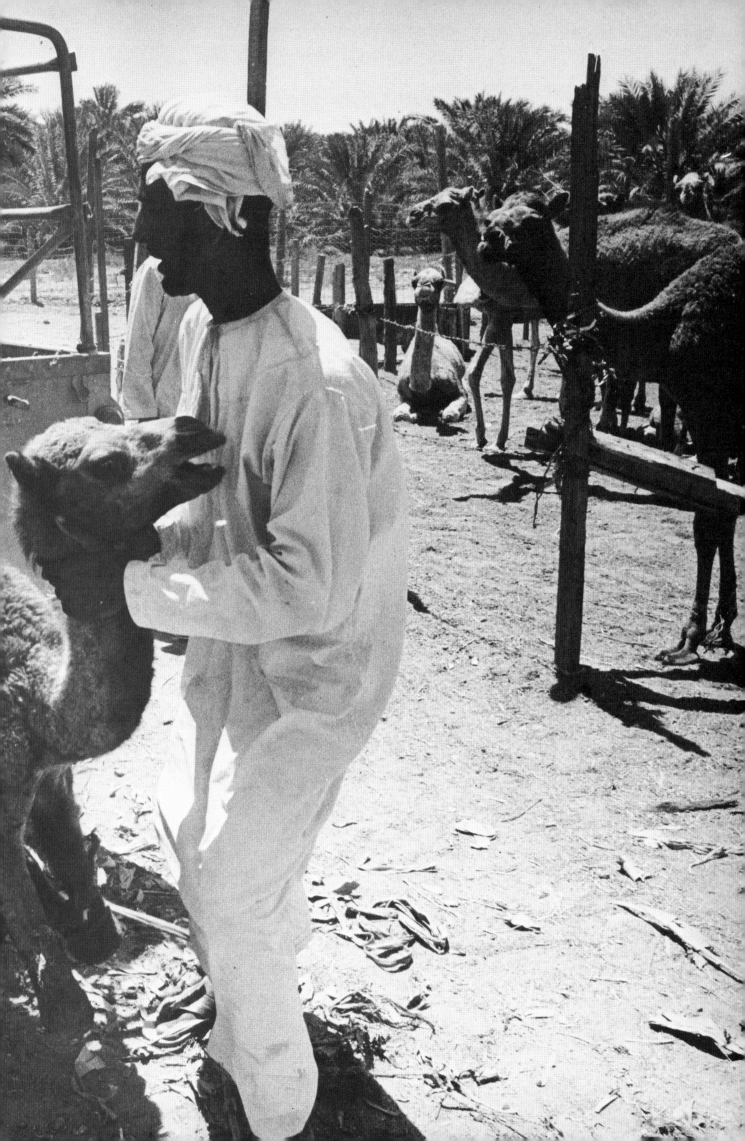

is a tremor in them when the animal couches down or rises up.

Next evening I saw a couching camel's throat being slit. It was for a wedding. Looking away I directed my eyes instead to the feet of the men who were rehearsing the dance that they would do on the next day. Yet all the time I know that on the far side of the tent the beast was falling to its feet and was presently being skinned. The tent itself was a beautiful vermilion and along its walls danced the shadows of the men and also the shadows of the seated men who passed the big water-pipe ponderously from one to another. It had all the beauty and the appointed stillness of a painting by Titian. As usual it was a male occasion. We knew it was a wedding because of the customary chain of fairy lights around the house pre-welcoming cousins and neighbours. We entered and after some slight conversation we were miraculously made welcome.

I was the only woman there but by now I was used to that and felt neither brave nor meek, just singular. In the light from two Tilley lamps under a vast orange tent fifty or sixty men sat around. They smoked a pipe, intoned and sometimes talked. Those faces and countenances looking like faces from time immemorial, with hollowed cheeks and eyes that looked out austerely and yet not without concupiscence. I wondered if they were as ignorant of my world as those who asked Mr Doughty if the moon might be seen in Western lands, or the number of eunuchs Queen Victoria had.

The bride-to-be was in her own home being decked by the women, some tending to her hair, some to her dress, and several to the engravings of henna which they stippled on her hands, her feet. The whole event had in it the elements of ritual, of strangeness, of beauty and of cruelty. Behind the tent the camel's throat being slit, slaughter for circumcision and slaughter for marriage. But we were invited back the next day and I was allowed to visit the bride. It was a funny scene. The real feast, the real dancing, the real chanting took place in the male quarters where the huge pans of food – rice and camel meat – were being passed around. Here the old men with those magnificent faces of inscrutability presided. Here cousins welcomed cousins while in the littler house sat the bride rather like a window dummy dripping with gold, sporting a white dress from London, a beehive hairdo and a smile! She was surrounded by women and squealing children and looking decidedly as if she would like the festivity to be over, as if she would like her husband to come and get her. The air in that room was hot and the only entertainment was a young girl doing a rather desperate amateur attempt at a belly-dance.

Later I asked the bride's handsome husband if he had in fact met his wife and he said if he told me there would be shame on her if anyone knew. I take it that he had met her but that change there, like change in Ireland, happens slowly and surreptitiously so as not to incur the wrath of the older people, so as not to jeopardize tradition.

It is of course chiefly by contrast – as Jung knew – that we perceive others. It only required a visit to the British Embassy to find that I was back in a world where abruptness, discourtesy and pseudo-authority were sadly in full sway. In short I was a nuisance. I received a galloping conversation from the Ambassador in which I was told that I was in a twentieth-century place, populated by twentieth-century people, that social life was a bit patchy, that everything was wonderful, that the pink and brown races mixed admirably, that he could not make appointments for me and that I would be a fool if I were to follow in the steps of Miss Linda Blandford by trying to do headline stuff.

I had to smile. My progress was such that I was in

grave danger of doing no stuff. There I was, simply armed with the blue and silver kit that said on the cover 'Where Dreams Come True', the recipient of several handshakes and as many sips of coffee, a mere writer in a total dilemma about what she should write. In fact emotionally barren. I thought of gold-diggers and their guests. I remembered the first morning when the young men in the Minister's office had asked what kind of book it was going to be, and I had said that I hardly knew and they had said that I was to think of the future and for the merest second we crossed mental swords. I had said that the future does not exist by itself alone, that the future must contain the past. They had smiled. One had said that if I needed anything to please call on him. I had listed all the people I would like to meet, all the places I would like to go, and he had put his two large brown arms up in front of him to deal with his four inhuman telephones. He had said that above all he would like me to be frank. Frank in expressing my needs. I had said that I wanted an audience with the Ruler and he had smiled at my audaciousness. It came. Much, much later.

Meanwhile I had gone to the office of a young Minister.

'We are not primitives,' he had said, in answer to my protestation about the jitters that my presence as a writer had created. He lifted the cording of his head-dress and threw it off like a naughty child, and then as he took off his head-dress I saw boyish curly hair. 'You do not have to love us but you need not dislike us.'

I said emotiveness was not on my agenda but that I wanted to know the people, soul speaking back to soul, cadence, truth, these things. In a grand gesture he threw open the window and pointed to the overbuilt city as he spoke of the ghosts of what he knew as a child – blue sea, fishermen, fish to live on, a few huts, a fortress and beyond the high dune and the marauding tribes. He said he would take me in hand. I think he meant it. As I left his room – it was eleven that night – the several telephones were ringing, the television was on and rebala music was being played from a desert peak. The new bookshelves were waiting for books. The mind as yet with so many millions of impressions to receive. A few days later I saw a photograph of the same Minister co-signing a document with the French Ambassador promising cooperation in historical excavations.

Yet to my eyes the breach with the past is radical. There is not only haste, there is amnesia. I do not say that the old men with the camel sticks who wait for the *majlis* each morning, patient, hoping to whisper in Sheikh Zayed's ear, I do not say that these men are oblivious of the past, but elsewhere the prevailing ethos is for haste, improvement and improvisation. The illiterate have to be made literate, a breakwater built for the harbour, flats built, mobile homes hauled in, sodium streetlights installed, a traffic system and a traffic sense developed, kerbstones put down, paving slabs, polythene greenhouses, feed-drips for the trees. In fact everything has to be done and the simple life is now a figment. But the other reason for discounting the past is that having made the incalculable leap from poverty and obscurity, it is impossible to look backwards. It is like bringing an old or dotty relation to a smart gathering. The future is the momentum.

Hegel identified the East with nature and saw the whole process of our civilization as an escape from nature. If he were alive today he would have to revise his thought. While I was there a group of children were asked by a newspaper to offer their suggestions as regards their homes in the year 2000. Power, gadgetry, depersonalization and science-fiction themes dominated. There were moving sidewalks, cars with atomic batteries, for the most part, planes instead of cars, and even rockets, there was transportation by hydro-electric power trains, by solar power trains, there was food in tablets or food from the tap or food from petrol, there was a magical arm that produced *anything*, there were houses that one travelled inside, there were magic buttons to do the work and robots to lay the table. A long way from the simplicity of the noble savage.

I little thought that it would be Franz Kafka that I would most think of when I was permitted to the palace of Sheikh Zayed's favourite wife Sheikha Fatima. He, more than any writer, knew the confoundedness of being invited to a throne room, of feeling forgotten except when it came to the handling of tea or a pastry, of being pregnant with the impression that very soon one will be noticed and that power will throw its beam on one and change the atmosphere radically.

There was a cluster of women, most of them veiled. The gilt tea trolley was weighed down with pastries and titbits and the prevailing smell was sandalwood. Their talking was so fervid, so ceaseless that now and then I ventured to ask what topics were being discussed to be told cursorily by the secretary that the topics were work, the improvement of the country and the progress of their children. I had prepared three questions but was told that Her Highness could not give them an answer at that moment since the answer must be 'culturally proper'. She had the advantage of being able to peer at me through the slits in her mask whereas I felt naked and as if I had simply come to pry.

I was sent to another room to write my questions down, so that they could be considered, mulled over, so that they could be answered adequately. The other room was also vast and there were the glass fruits, English seaside scenes, the lion skins, the photograph of His Highness and the numerous photographs of hawks.

After I had handed over my written questions I waited for the audience to come to an end. Two more hours passed. Perhaps the key is that having waited so long, so endlessly and so patiently themselves they expect me to wait too. Here for me was the crux of it all and to my mind the biggest cultural conflict – the difference between movement and stasis, between concealment and self-expression, between being a woman of the East and a woman of the West.

Had I been there longer something might have happened. Gradually, or suddenly, we might have talked. It is not a case of the new broom sweeping clean with them, but rather 'beware stranger'. Some Bedouin woman of the past had asked Mr Burckhardt to whom he had lent his wife while he was travelling. No such ignorant thralldom pervades today's thinking but a quality does persist and it is the quality of reserve. I doubt that one of these women at court is secretly compiling a diary that will astonish a future generation. Such a thing would represent dishonour, both to her tribe and to herself.

The theme and torments of any modern Western woman's novel would be deemed irrelevant here. I am not in a position to say whether one day such novels will be accepted, read, mulled over, or whether indeed that would constitute a leap of the imagination. The fundament of thought, behaviour, action and non-action is so different that they may never need to read those books. The emergence may have to be different. Yet I would like to see a poet emerge, one who would proclaim the virtues and the vices of her country, one who would attempt the unattemptable, and set it on the shelf of literature alongside all the other poems, written by all the other poets, of every creed, every nationality and every denomination.

To a stranger the chief thing about the Ruler Sheikh Zayed is his powerful regal presence. It is magnetic and undoubtedly sexual in direct contrast to our conversation

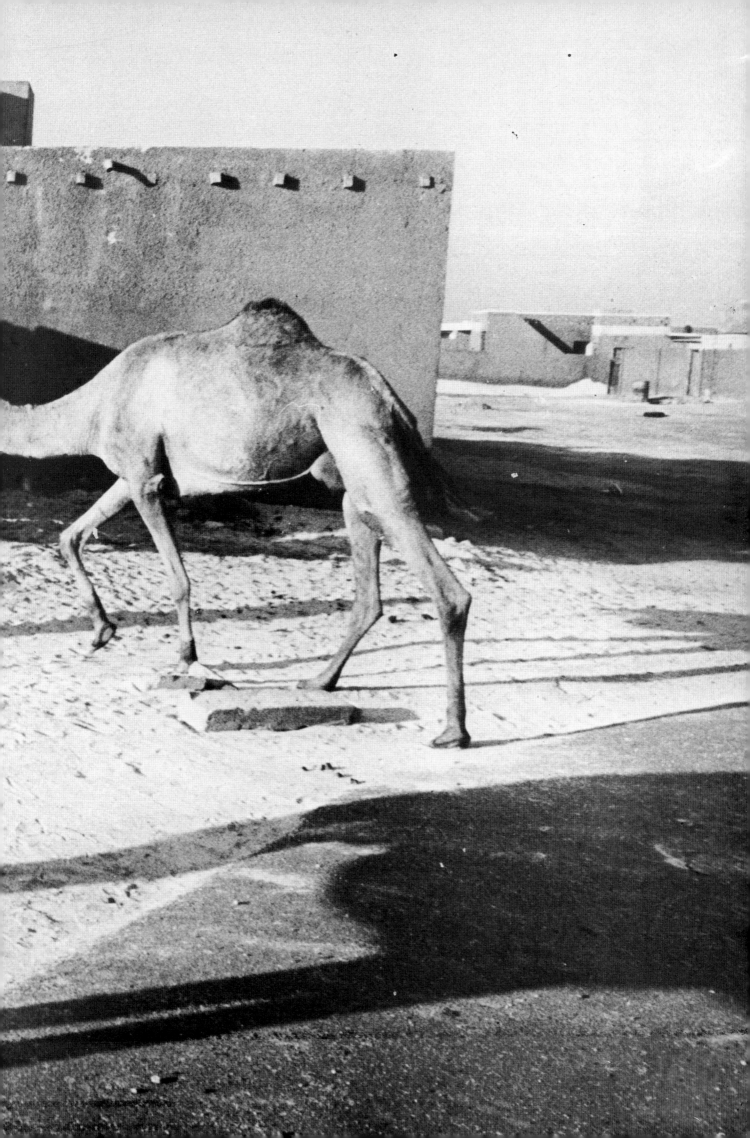

which is formal, baroque and excelling in social fervour.

As he came from the wings through an open door I saw attendants move to one side and felt that hush and flutter that one witnesses in Shakespeare's kingly plays. Here in the twentieth century a glimpse of the grand mechanism of power, while on the staircase of history those who advise, those who watch, those who flatter, those who bow and those who wait. His succession too was in the tradition of the direful, except that he deposed his brother in a bloodless coup. His father before him was murdered while he was still a boy and the story goes that his mother, Sheikha Salama, was a profound influence on him and his brothers. She imbued them with thrift and an abhorrence of the inevitable bloody coup, and it seems was both enlightened and unafraid to voice her terms within a male dominion. But then mothers wield more power than do wives!

As he moved forward some of the old men and he touched noses. Then he saw me and took my hand and the grip was heartening. His face is long, beautiful and enticing. One wants to touch it, or trace it, or hold it. One of those faces that defy the ravages of time. His eyes are matchless. Not simply beautiful, like those of, say, Rudolph Valentino, but searching. His eyes are searchlights. There is the merest droop to his left lid. He is wearing a brown robe edged with gold braid and his head is covered with a white headpiece, but for the most part he emanates a simplicity. A simplicity of appearance that is. His mind has been trained not to give quick or darting answers, and he combines a politician's genius for not answering simply with the Arab ability for mystique and circumlocutoriness. There is no doubt but that he loves and cares for his own people, and that the love, if you like the adoration, is reciprocal. Everywhere they point to his achievements, and constantly one is told that he does not keep the money for himself, but doles it out. Visitors get costly gifts, countries get foreign aid, and his own people get free education, medicine, maintenance of all sorts.

His age is a bit of a secret, but he must be nearing sixty. There is a heartening austerity about him. Emerson said, 'The hero is he who is immovably centred.' In that sense, Sheikh Zayed is a hero. But he is not an intellectual, and he is not open. Sigmund Freud would be hard put to get an inkling of his subconscious. He has had many wives and over a dozen children. He is moody, given at times to the most ravishing informality, and at other times he cannot be found for days, having returned to his native shore, the desert. Yet he loves agriculture and husbandry. In the male/female quota that every man is endowed with (and every woman), he seems to have been given an exquisite balance of each. It may be that he is not a brooding man but yet he emanates a reflectiveness and a gravity. He is master of any situation and without doubt a father-figure. Poverty, heat, hardship and desert loneliness have honed him well. In the world outside, he and his people are on the crest of a wave. The future is of course one that is bound to bring change because the opposite means ennui and stagnation. At the moment they are busy building, businessing, drilling and dealing, but at the same time some of his subjects are now in England and are now in America, absorbing different ideas, and when they go back they will surely find a cultural gulf. I do not know or even conjecture what that change will be, but the Sheikh's ruling son will have a harder time than his father and will perhaps not have his father's metal, having been more exposed to wealth, to flattery, to cars, boats, yachts and the sweetmeats of power.

I asked him what qualities he most respected in a man. His answer was the ability to live and co-live with the people around him, in short not to be isolated from his nation or his people. Applying the same question to what was best in a woman he smiled somewhat and said that man's knowledge of woman is limited. Naturally I could not let that pass. But when it came to who were his heroes I felt that his heroes were himself. It was there that he made the point that though a man may seem limited to the outside world he knows best what is right for his own country, and that people who are outside the house ought not to criticize the owner of the house as they do not know the facts and the situation! It was perhaps a reminder to me myself of how I saw the place and how outside it I was. I did not have their commitment, and how could I?

As I was leaving I saw him in the long throne room surrounded by the men who had come, as they do each day, to tell their worries. A man was whispering in his ear, and he was listening, with that attentiveness that is particular to him. I thought of the confessional, then the psychiatrist's couch, and I thought that, yes, I would like to go each day, and whisper my worries in his ear. But I am a woman, and he could not listen to me, at least not in public. Long after I left him I read a book about him in which he said that the most important quality in a man was *hazz* – good luck.

Mr Thesiger said his journey in the desert had been like a drink of clean, nearly tasteless water. My own journey there was more like a small cup of bitter coffee. Mr Thesiger also said that perhaps he was the last of the travellers since future visitors would move by car and would listen to the wireless. He could have been speaking of me. My journey was like the one on the helicopter – marvellous, dizzying, rapid and unnerving.

I can only think on a human everyday scale, and when I think of Abu Dhabi, the essays in the kit book or the Minister's persuasiveness have slipped my memory, and I think of small things such as Sheikh Zayed's aide coming to my hotel the next day to ask if I had not thought his replies most engaging. I think of the cold, air-conditioned dining rooms, the unleavened bread, the paste made of sesame seed, sun, the deck-chairs around the swimming pool, then the deserted deck-chairs, the falcon on somebody's shoulder as I sat for dinner, a grey falcon with a red cloth pad over its eyes. I think of the rubble outside the apartment blocks and inside a surprising amount of grandeur and sophistication. I think of the heat. I think of the wedding I saw, the men chanting and stamping their feet while over in the other house the bedecked bride sat with the women and waited for her husband to come and claim her. I think of the desert in all its raiment of colours. I think of the profusion of red flowers like lanterns in Sheikh Zayed's garden. A little bit of England. Even birdsong. I think of the Indian waiter who said that his life was like the life of a soldier in war - work, eat and sleep. On his free day he played cricket with the club. His sister had a little temple in her bedroom, a little homemade outfit with joss-sticks and petals. I think of the gardener from Saudi Arabia who, as he pruned the date trees, looked across the sea to where his wife was. A gardener in Saudi Arabia being a novelty. I think of all the people that I met but did not meet because it takes a long time to discover and know one another. It takes a lifetime. My outside impression is that they were simple, hospitable, elusive, touchy, aching to be loved and undoubtedly smarting under the recent imputation of being licentious.

I feel fonder of Abu Dhabi than when I was there, chiefly because I have not the heat or their protractedness to contend with. Travel, as Richard Burton knew, is finally wearying because we find each race wedded to its own opinions which they do not relinquish unless they are conquered. I venture to say that they are caught in the modern fever of having constantly to be doing something lest they be accused of doing nothing. And of course they are fervid in their aspirations to be a people to be reckoned with. But I also think that oil, like good looks, does not last for ever, and if they are farseeing now they will build a society where the spiritual and meditative side of life, once nourished by the desert, is renourished by its only other source – Art. I agree with Oscar Wilde that it is through art and through art only that we can realize our perfection, through art and through art only that we can shield ourselves from the sordid perils of actual existence. Yes, to build a society that does not live by bread alone but one that sends roots down into the desert, to those hidden places where the camel bones and the Sumerian fragments are said to reside. That is my enjoinder.